ARNESON and POLITICS

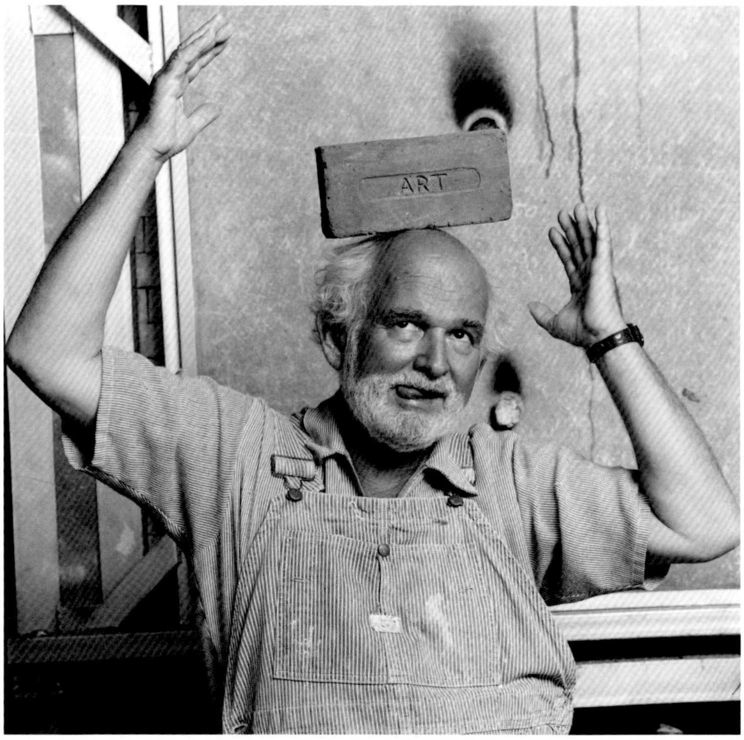

Robert Arneson, 1986

ARNESON *and* POLITICS

A Commemorative Exhibition

STEVEN A. NASH

The Fine Arts Museums of San Francisco

POLITICS

and

ARNESON

ARNESON *and* **POLITICS**

A Commemorative Exhibition

THE FINE ARTS MUSEUMS OF SAN FRANCISCO

M.H. de Young Memorial Museum

2 June *through* 15 August 1993

Publication of this catalogue was made possible through the generosity of the John Berggruen Gallery, San Francisco.

The exhibition is organized by The Fine Arts Museums of San Francisco and made possible by support from Rena Bransten, Morgan Flagg, Frumkin/Adams Gallery, John Jones, Byron Meyer, and Ruth and Ted Nash.

Library of Congress Catalogue Card No. 93-71398

ISBN 0-88401-077-5

Editing and production supervision by the Publications Department, The Fine Arts Museums of San Francisco

Photography in the catalogue courtesy of M. Lee Fatherree, Abe Frajndlich, Michele Maier, Joe Nobody, Schopplein Studio, and Ken Showell

Printing by Woods Lithographics, Phoenix, Arizona

Designed by Leif Eric Arneson, San Francisco

"My involvement in the creation of this catalogue is dedicated to the memory of my father, Robert C. Arneson, whose creative spirit is all the inspiration that I could ever ask for."

Front and back covers: **California Artist**, 1983 *(cat. no. 11)*

Contents

Preface

When Robert Arneson died in November of 1992, he was only sixty-two years old. Yet, for over thirty years he had been recognized as one of the Bay Area's leading artists and teachers and one of the most important ceramic sculptors in America. His loss is deeply felt by all who knew him and grew to love his work. We communally share the sad deprivation of future works that, no matter where his career might have led him, would undoubtedly have been just as exciting and revealing as those from the first thirty remarkable years of productivity.

Arneson is best known as the comic gagster of modern sculpture. From the Pop Art objects of the early sixties through his many self-portrait busts and caricatured depictions of others, he poked fun at himself, at the art world, and at pomposity and narrow-mindedness wherever he found them. His wit, however, always had a probing quality and an element of bitter truth. In the works that Steven Nash has selected for the present exhibition, humor still can be found, but it yields in importance to the political message delivered, ranging from mordant commentary and warnings about topical issues to outright moral rage. These are some of the hardest hitting works that Arneson ever produced and show how strongly he felt his responsibilities as an artist/observer. Coincidentally, they reveal that his gifts as a draftsman and painter, not generally as widely recognized, are equal to those he displayed in sculpture.

At a time in contemporary art when more and more young artists are dealing with social themes and political commentary, partly out of a sense of desperation with life in modern America, partly as a way out of the formalist quandaries of previous generations, Arneson's political sculptures and drawings have a kind of patriarchal authority. Along with a few other artists such as Leon Golub and George Segal, Arneson was exploring political narrative when it was far from fashionable and, in fact, posed a challenge to prevailing trends toward minimalism and conceptual art. In a career based on a willingness to buck convention and stand alone, this is another sign of Arneson's stubborn independence.

The current exhibition and its accompanying catalogue are the creation of Steven A. Nash, Associate Director and Chief Curator at The Fine Arts Museums of San Francisco. The fresh perspective they offer on a particularly important aspect of Arneson's work is a welcomed first step in what will undoubtedly be a lengthy process of reassessment and evaluation of Arneson's contribution to modern art. The project would not have been possible without the close cooperation of Sandra Shannonhouse and her staff and the generosity of numerous donors, including John and Gretchen Berggruen, Rena Bransten, Ruth and Ted Nash, Byron Meyer, Morgan Flagg, John Jones, and the Frumkin/Adams Gallery. We thank all of them as well as the lenders and many staff members of our Museums who enthusiastically supported the exhibition. This show represents another step in the increasing commitment of The Fine Arts Museums of San Francisco to play an active role in the contemporary art life of the Bay Area. That it should take place at the M.H. de Young Memorial Museum is highly appropriate, since Arneson had one of his first museum exhibitions at the de Young in 1962.

HARRY S. PARKER III
Director of Museums

Acknowledgments

When Robert Arneson's portrait bust of George Moscone came to The Fine Arts Museums more than a year ago on long-term loan, the idea occurred of organizing a small exhibition based on *Portrait of George* and related works. With Arneson's untimely death several months later, the possibility of an exhibition in his honor took on new meaning, and I suggested, and Harry Parker quickly approved, a show based on the political themes in Arneson's work, with *Portrait of George* as one of its focal points. Although Arneson devoted increasing artistic emphasis to political and social commentary starting around 1980-81, no exhibition or publication had ever provided an overview of this key body of work, and many of the sculptures, paintings, and drawings most central to the theme had never before been exhibited in the Bay Area. It was decided to act quickly so as to include the project in the Museums' 1992-93 schedule.

Because of the unusually short working period that resulted, the assistance of those who supported and contributed to the exhibition became especially critical. Most notable was the unstinting cooperation of Sandra Shannonhouse, Arneson's wife of twenty years and fellow artist. Sandra supplied and arranged for many of the loans for the show, patiently answered myriad questions about Arneson and his work, and provided much good advice and moral support throughout the organizational process. The show simply could not have taken place without her help and that of her assistant, Pat Thomas, who also gave freely of her time and knowledge and was especially diligent in assembling the many photographs for the catalogue.

For underwriting the handsomely produced exhibition catalogue and providing help with loans, we are deeply grateful to John and Gretchen Berggruen. Other donors include Morgan Flagg, Byron Meyer, Rena Bransten, John Jones, Ruth and Ted Nash, and the Frumkin/Adams Gallery. Their help came as an expression of devotion to Arneson and his work and is very much appreciated. To the lenders to the exhibition we offer special thanks for parting with beloved objects so that we could share them with our public. In addition to Sandra Shannonhouse, the list of generous lenders includes the John Berggruen Gallery, John and Earlene Taylor, the Riva Yares Gallery, Trish Bransten, the Dorothy Goldeen Gallery, Frumkin/Adams Gallery, the John Natsoulas Gallery, Ross and Paula Turk, Brian Gross Fine Art, Rene di Rosa, Gerson Bakar, Claire E. Flagg, the San Francisco Museum of Modern Art, Dodie and John Rosekrans, and the Foster Goldstrom family.

Leif Eric Arneson designed this catalogue as a special tribute to his father, and we are particularly grateful to him for both the dedication and the creative energy he brought to the project.

Numerous members of the art community generously shared information with me about Arneson and his art. In particular I would like to thank Wanda Hansen, Diana Fuller, Brian Gross, John Natsoulas, Riva Yares, Dorothy Goldeen, Mady Jones, Richard Reisman, Manuel Neri, Rene di Rosa, Signe Mayfield, Ross Turk, and Rena Bransten. The fine catalogue that Neal Benezra wrote for the Arneson retrospective of 1986 was a constantly valuable reference tool. Within our own staff, many individuals contributed importantly to the "fast track" production of this exhibition, helping to ensure its success: Ann Karlstrom, Director of Publications; Pamela Forbes, Editor of *Triptych* magazine; my assistant, Suzy Peterson; Bill White, Exhibitions Designer; Ron Rick of the Design Department; Elisabeth Cornu, Objects Conservator; and Sonya Knudsen of the Registration Department. Harry Parker, Director of Museums, supported the project from its inception. Last, but with special emphasis, I would like to thank Mary Maggini, Curator of the Runnymede Sculpture Farm, who generously donated her time to work on the catalogue bibliography and chronology, thus ensuring their timely completion.

Steven A. Nash
Associate Director/Chief Curator

POLITICAL COMMITMENT IN OUR TIMES MEANS LOGICALLY — NO ART, NO LITERATURE. A GREAT MANY PEOPLE, HOWEVER, FIND IT POSSIBLE TO HANG AROUND IN THE SPACE BETWEEN ART AND POLITICAL ACTION.

ROBERT MOTHERWELL *and* HAROLD ROSENBERG, 1947 [1]

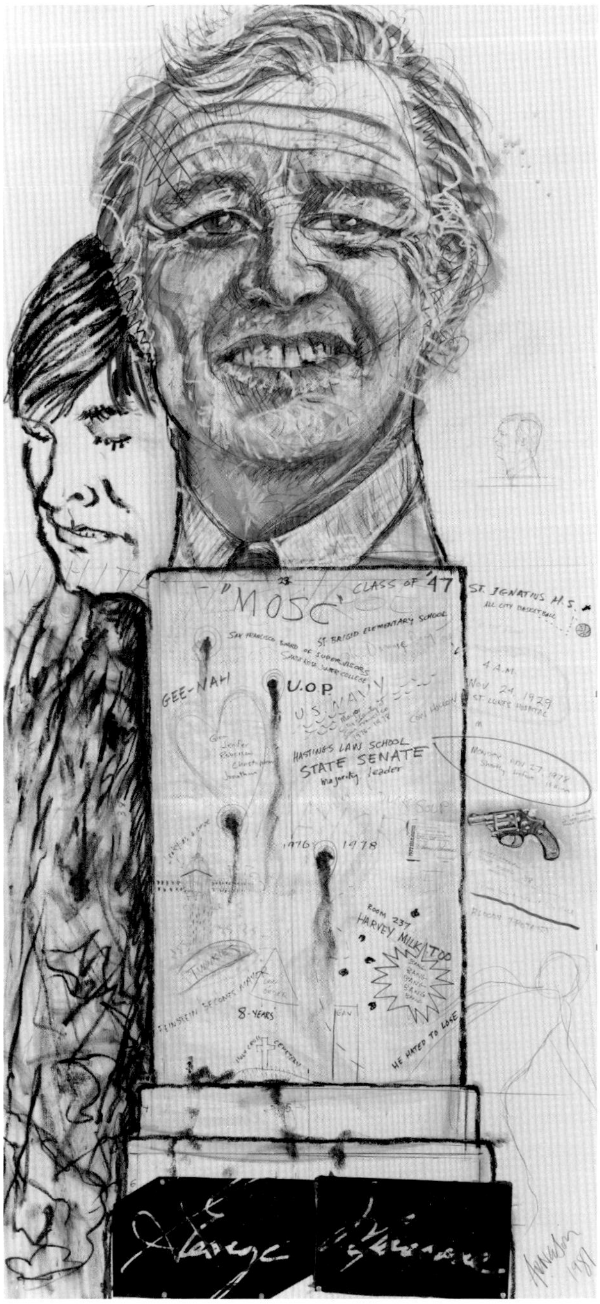

VERTICAL GEORGE, 1981
Cat. no. 4

THOSE ENGAGED IN THE BUSINESS OF SOCIETY CAN HAVE LITTLE UNDERSTANDING OF THE FRUSTRATIONS AND ANGER OF ARTISTS DEPRIVED OF A VOICE IN THEIR COUNTRY'S AFFAIRS, WHOSE RADICAL ART WAS GRADUALLY APPROPRIATED BY A CONSUMER CULTURE, AND WHOSE ATTEMPTS TO USE NORMAL CHANNELS OF PROTEST WERE LOOKED ON AS SUBVERSIVE . . . .

From an ad in the New York Times *of* 27 *June* 1965 *signed by* 500 *artists*

In Robert Arneson's irreverent, sometimes caustic art, humor and polemic hold equal sway. His reputation, of course, was built on the former. Best known for the persona of "loko klown" that he cultivated throughout his life,[2] Arneson relentlessly poked fun at both himself and others while pushing modern sculpture in new stylistic directions. For more than thirty years, he lampooned the pomposity and prejudices of individuals and institutions alike through boisterous, punning, superbly crafted, but jarringly funky sculptures that personify the no-holds-barred tradition of Northern California ceramics.

Ironically, the early success he enjoyed became an impediment to the understanding of his later development. Behind Arneson's gagster wit and faux naive posturing was a deeply perceptive intelligence that forced his work beyond the satire his audience came to expect into areas of serious thematic concern rarely visited by other twentieth-century sculptors. Whether expressed through irony or in more confrontational terms, these concerns embrace a range of issues, from entrenched prejudice against ceramic art, to critical agendas such as eastern attitudes toward West Coast artists, to urgent social and political problems. Arneson never lost his wry outlook on the human condition, even during his battles with cancer. As his career progressed, however, and he became more confident of the darkly expressive voice in his sculpture and drawings, the serious side of his art moved increasingly to the forefront, sometimes erupting with ferocious intensity. Work of this nature often caught critics and supporters off guard. It remains unsettling today.

Arneson refutes the claim that modern art has no conscience. For more than thirty years he explored a mutable figurative vocabulary that fulfilled his intention "to treat ceramics as another art process" in which "we had to deal with ideas and content."[3] Some of his most hard-hitting content came in the arena of politics. Never a radical in his own political actions but always cognizant of issues of social justice and humanitarian policy, he took aim at one shibboleth after another. Political figures appear in his art in many guises, from the heroic to the mock-heroic and heinous. The sanctioned brutality and destructiveness of war, and especially the threat of nuclear holocaust, were dominant themes, as was social violence through forces of racism, hatred, and censorship. Also important to Arneson throughout his career were the politics of the artist and the art market and the strange mixtures of mythification and exploitation that often intrude. Much of his work can be appreciated for its gentler qualities of cleverness and inventive handling of color and form. Its more challenging side, however, seen in the current exhibition, adds important dimension to our understanding of Arneson as a person and a citizen/artist.

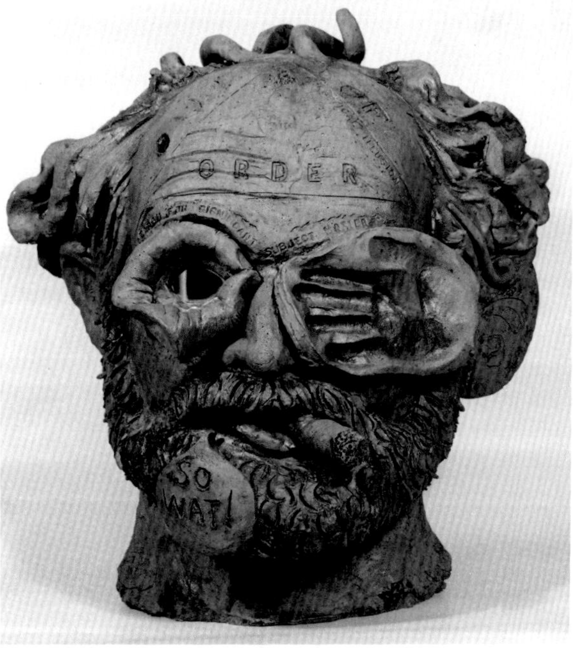

fig. 1 **SEARCH FOR SIGNIFICANT SUBJECT MATTER**, 1974
Stoneware, 30 in.

Mildura Arts Center, Australia

Arneson's concern with content in his art (one of his best-known early pieces was the *Search for Significant Subject Matter* from 1974, *fig.* 1) came only after a lengthy apprenticeship in which he refined his technical skills through work with traditional ceramic forms. His training at the California College of Arts and Crafts (B.A., 1954) was general, and at the time of his M.F.A. show at Mills College (1959), his ceramics still adhered strictly to a Japanese-inspired crafts tradition. Soon he began to experiment more daringly with a rough, organic style of improvisational abstraction influenced by Peter Voulkos, who had moved from Los Angeles to Berkeley in 1958, and Joan Miró. By 1963 he had developed the personal brand of whimsical, Pop Art ceramic objects such as toasters, toilets, and typewriters for which he became well known.

These works appropriate mundane icons of consumerist society in a wry commentary on modern living and on the new Duchampian boundaries of art. As much as they represent a western migration of eastern Pop Art sensibilities, they have a gutsy, physical, often scatological quality that separates the elegant crudity of Arneson's humor and way of working from the cooler, more formal approach of his East Coast counterparts.

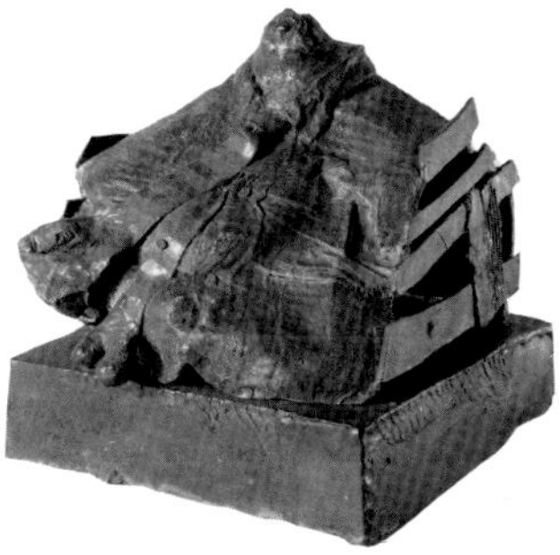

fig. 2 **THE CRITIC**, 1964
Bronze, 19 1/4 x 16 1/2 x 18 in.

Estate of the artist

Toaster, from 1965, is typical of Arneson's subverting play of images, which twists meaning and undercuts expectation. From the top of an ordinary household toaster protrude four fingers. At first the object seems like another straightforward Pop joke, but attention eventually comes to the swastika added on the end. Suddenly, horrific associations of the Holocaust and human incineration intrude. Arneson's humor often sears as much as it amuses.

Another aspect of the artist's early political thinking finds expression in *The Critic* of 1964 (*fig.* 2). This bronze, headless sculpture, with a pair of testicles attached to the end of the flopping tie, speaks in typically mordant terms of Arneson's disdain for art critics and writers, who have characteristically discounted the importance of ceramic art in the field of modern sculpture. Numerous works from the seventies expand upon this dialogue with critics and art criticism and embrace as well the parallel theme of the artist as misunderstood or abused seer. *Assassination of a Famous Nut Artist,* 1972,[4] gives warning, although not too seriously, of one of the more extreme denouements for any artist who probes too far into the public psyche. A drawing from 1978, *Double Mask: Wearing a Happy Face,*[5] shows melancholia concealed behind a happy exterior, a characterization of artistic personality going back, for example, to the work of Watteau, Daumier, and Picasso.

The well-known *Klown* of 1978 (*fig.* 3) is a particularly biting self-caricature of the artist doubling as slapstick entertainer. In *A Question of Measure,* 1978,[6] Arneson substitutes in the self-consciously mundane format of a ceramic plate his own pudgy, all-too-vulnerable body for Leonardo's idealized Man as the measure of all things. Carrying this imagery further, *Casualty in the Art Realm,* 1979 (*fig.* 4), bears the imprint of the artist's

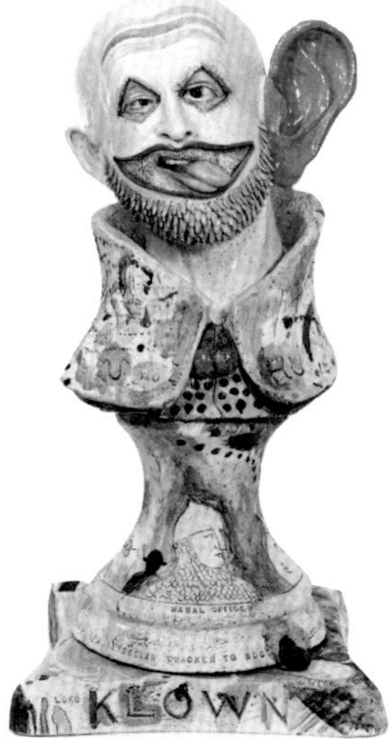

fig. 3 **KLOWN**, 1978
Glazed ceramic, 37 x 19 x 19 in.

Des Moines Art Center, Coffin Fine Arts Trust

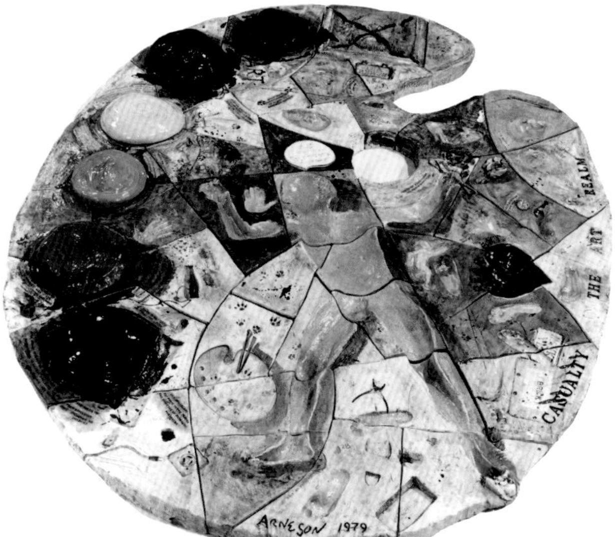

fig. 4 **CASUALTY IN THE ART REALM**, 1979
Glazed ceramic, 8 x 97 x 132 in.

Palm Springs Desert Museum

body spread-eagled like a murder victim on a huge ceramic palette, providing a statement about the many hostile forces in art world politics. It is also an uncanny prophecy of the pain that Arneson would suffer just two years later over the rejection of the commissioned portrait bust of George Moscone. In light of the very real struggles Arneson faced in advancing his career, these works can be seen not as paranoiac or overly defensive, but rather as part humor and part poignant, personal testimony.

In many ways, *Portrait of George* (cat. no. 2) marks a turning point in Arneson's work, particularly in regard to its politicization. The piece was his second public commission and his largest sculpture to date. What started as an attempt at respectful public art, however, turned instead into a cause célèbre of philistinism that reinforced Arneson's innate skepticism toward the public's understanding of his work and unlocked the more darkly expressive side of his creativity. Pushed onto political ground, he began to explore it through one theme after another with a stridency never before so sustained.

The story is now well known of the commission of *Portrait of George* in 1981 for San Francisco's new Moscone Convention Center, its eventual rejection as too disrespectful and controversial by the City's Art Commission and Mayor Dianne Feinstein, and the public pillorying of Arneson in local newspapers.[7] The outcry over the sculpture centered not necessarily on the bust itself, which many may have seen as too cartoonish, but which nevertheless captures through its characterization and brilliant colors the presence of George Moscone with snapshot immediacy. Controversy focused instead on the base. Through such symbols as bloody bullet holes, the imprint of a gun, and a phallic Twinkie, it aggravated the still fresh memory of Dan White's shooting of Moscone and Supervisor Harvey Milk and his attorney's invocation of the infamous junk-food or "Twinkie" defense. Blatantly referencing historical fact, Arneson misjudged the degree of public sensitivity surviving over events that had rocked the community. During the ensuing uproar, the considerable merits of the sculpture itself were almost entirely overshadowed.

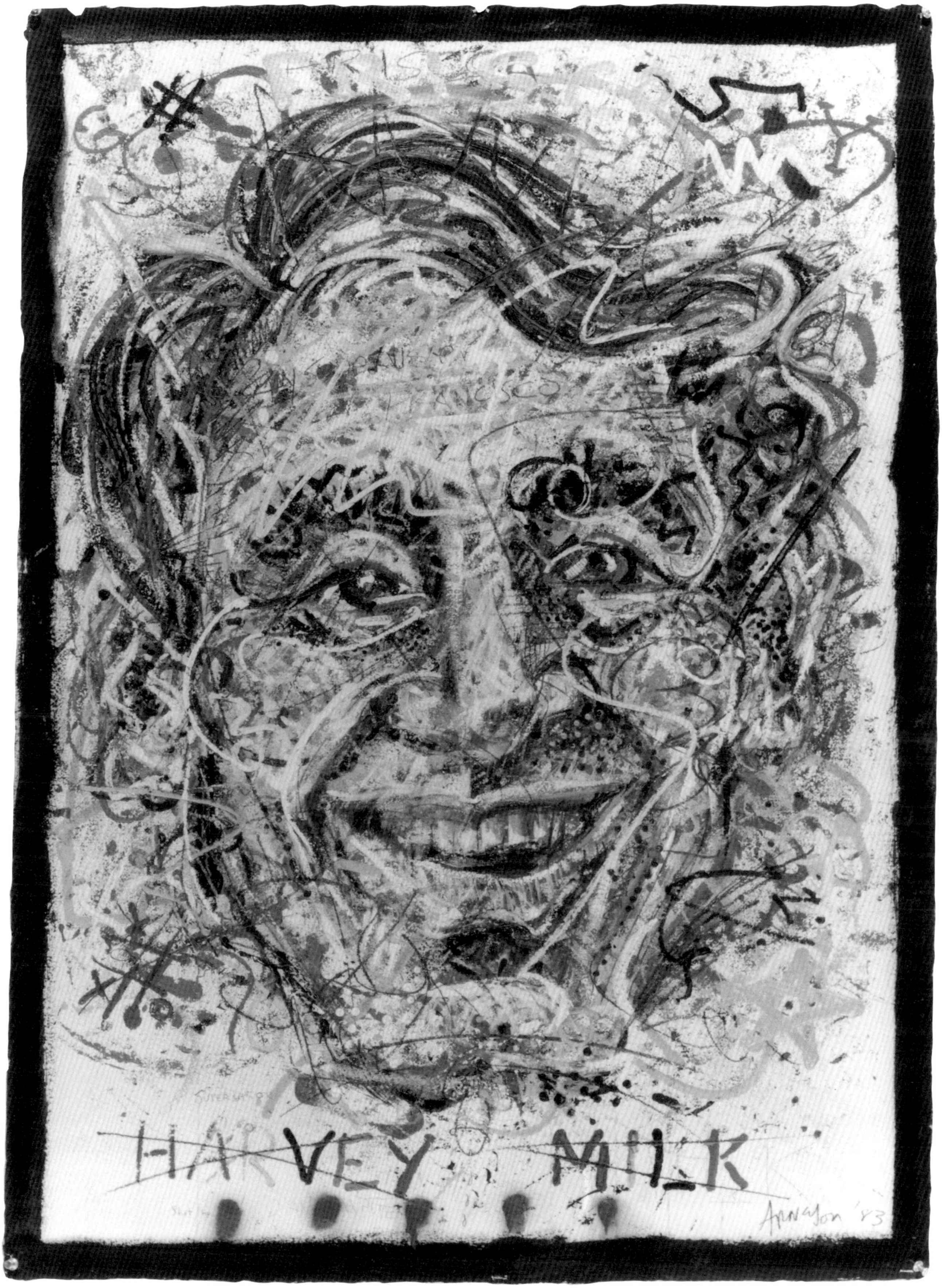

HARVEY MILK, 1983
Cat. no. 10

PORTAIT OF GEORGE, 1981
Cat. no. 2

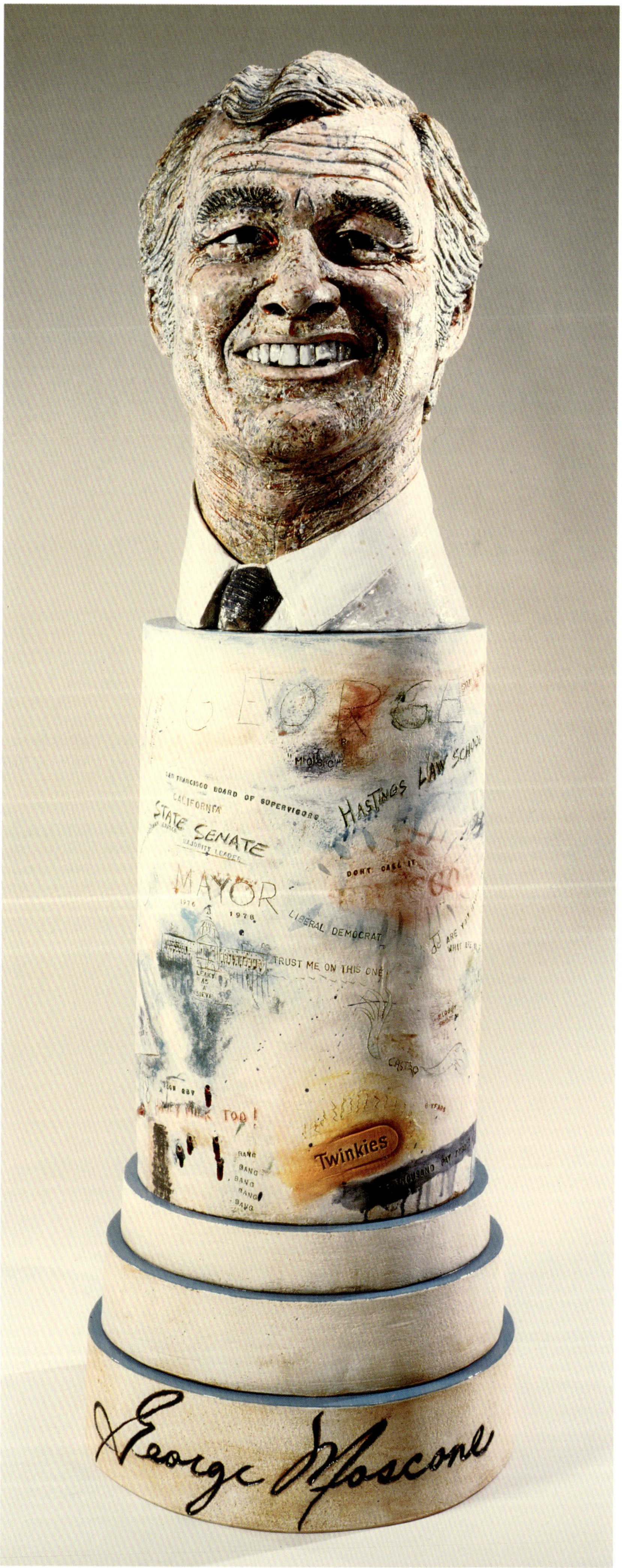

The most perceptive observer of these events was art critic Thomas Albright, who had long been a supporter of Arneson. He wrote soon after:

> **"THE SCULPTURE AS A WHOLE WAS CHARACTERISTIC OF ARNESON'S LARGER-THAN-LIFE CERAMIC PORTRAITURE AND SELF-PORTRAITURE, IN WHICH A MORE OR LESS LITERAL LIKENESS IS USUALLY ACCOMPANIED BY ATTRIBUTES OF THE SUBJECT'S VOCATION, AS WELL AS MORE PERSONAL MEMENTOS . . . .**
>
> **WHILE SCARCELY A GREAT WORK OF SCULPTURE, AND SURELY NOT A TRANSCENDENT ONE, ARNESON'S BUST OF THE ASSASSINATED MAYOR NEVERTHELESS AMOUNTED TO AN EXTRAORDINARILY COMPELLING, VITAL AND HIGHLY-CHARGED WORK OF PUBLIC ART . . . [THAT] ADDS UP TO A POWERFUL PICTURE OF THE TIMES . . . .**
>
> **IT IS A WORK THAT ACTUALLY PROMPTED A BROAD SEGMENT OF THE PUBLIC TO THINK AND DEBATE, AS DISTINCT FROM THE MILDLY APPROVING BUT BASICALLY INDIFFERENT REACTION TO THE MORE INNOCUOUS SORT OF EMBELLISHMENTS GENERALLY FOUND IN PUBLIC EDIFICES."**[8]

GEORGE MOSCONE, 1981
Cat. no. 3

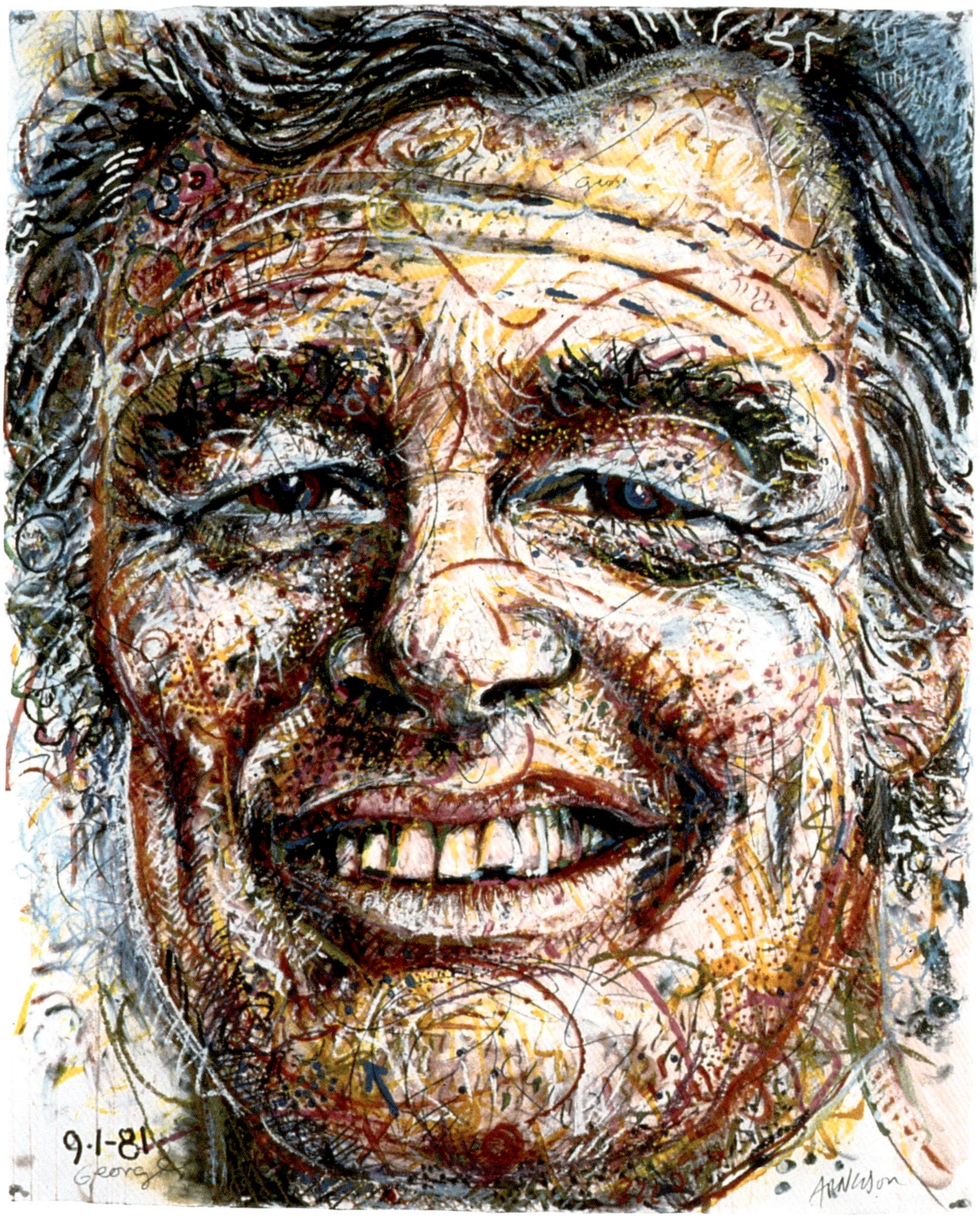

With greater distance from the painful events surrounding it, the bust can now be seen as much more than just a period piece, primarily of local interest. In its monumentality and vivid literalism mixed with the synthesizing quality of a Pop Art icon, *Portrait of George* translates transient details of life into something lasting and timeless. It does far greater honor to the energy and humanity of its subject than would be even remotely possible through the type of official portrait that City administrators may have wished they had commissioned. In purely visual terms, it is a remarkable object. The ancient sculptural tradition of a head on a pedestal takes a startlingly contemporary turn, with the upward thrust of the tapered base culminating in the colossal bust, whose strong modeling and bright splashes of color give the sculpture unnerving impact. The glazes in the face meld from a distance into lifelike realism, but up close, the abstract quality of speckled and dripped patterns shows a combination of improvisation and control that foretells the free-wheeling handling of paint and glaze that Arneson later exercised in outright homage to Jackson Pollock. Perhaps not his greatest work, *Portrait of George* nevertheless stands as a major milestone in Arneson's career.

Arneson did not take lightly his ensuing fall from grace. The scorn he absorbed fed his innate cynicism about the relationship between artists and society, and a series of works from 1981 and 1982 explored with anger and mock contrition the frustration and disappointment he felt. *Portrait of the Artist as a Clever Old Dog* (cat. no. 5) is a drawing for a sculpture of the same title, which shows the artist's head with woeful expression on the shaggy-coated body of a dog, his food dish inscribed "Bob" nearby. He sits in an area befouled with his own lumpy turds, as if this were the position to which he was consigned

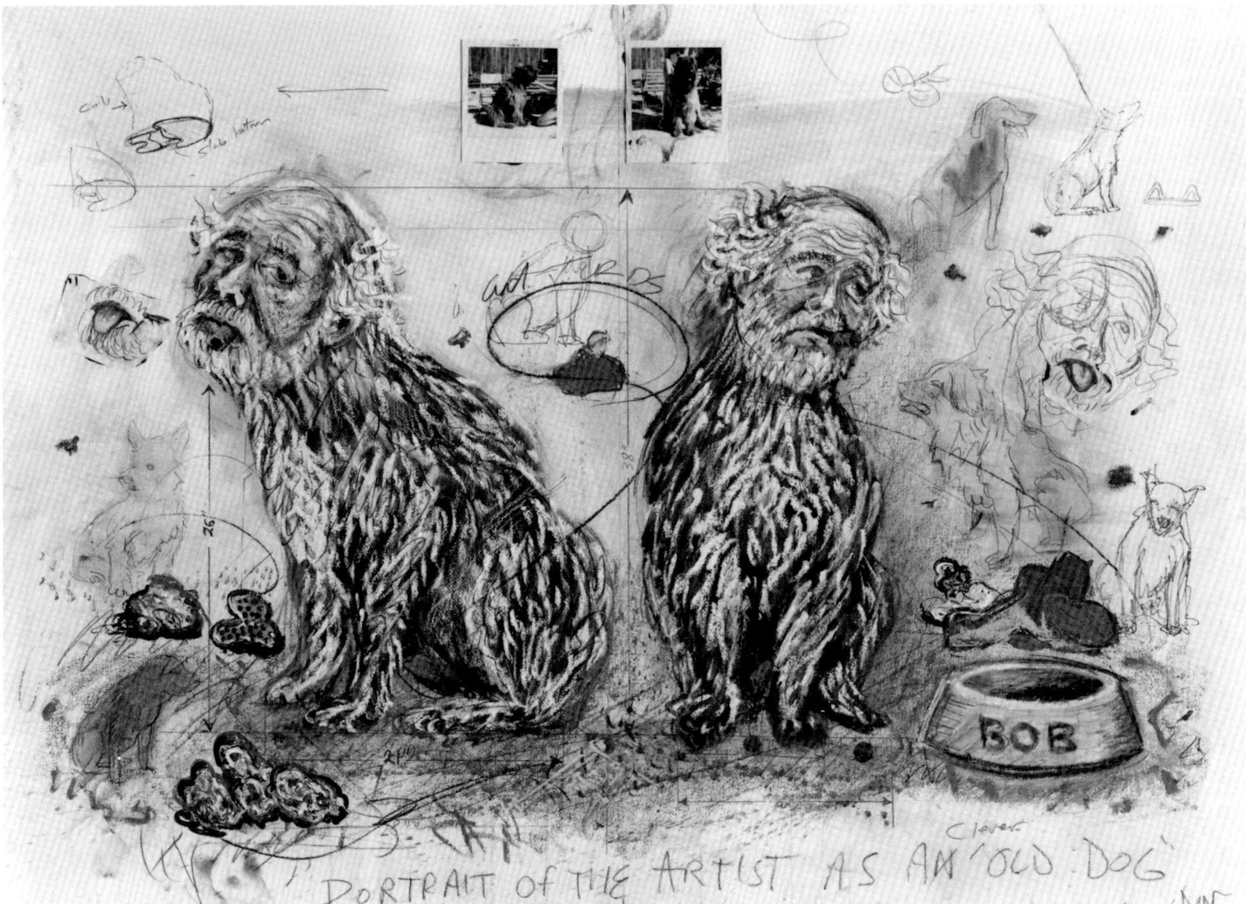

PORTAIT OF THE ARTIST AS A CLEVER OLD DOG, 1981
Cat. no. 5

EYE OF THE BEHOLDER, 1982

Cat. no. 7

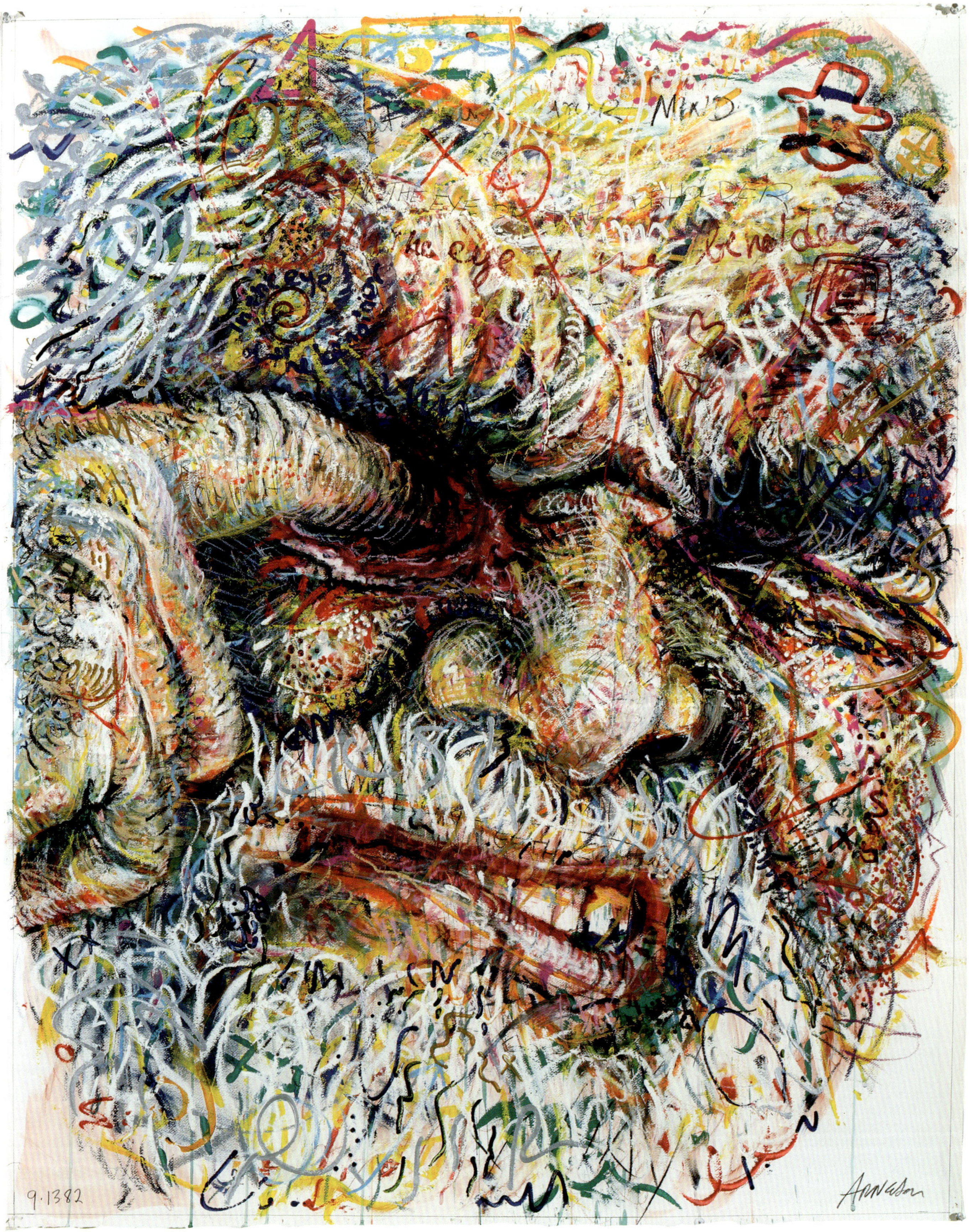

for life. *Eye of the Beholder* (cat. no. 7) is a self-portrait bursting with the frenetic energy of whiplash strokes and rich overlays of calligraphy and color that characterize Arneson's draftsmanship and painting style at their best. He shows himself, however, grimacing horribly from the pain of the finger he pokes into his own eye, an indication that this badboy of the art world has stuck it to himself again.

China Doll of 1982,[9] the smirking, pure white, ceramic portrait of Dianne Feinstein, projects with controlled anger Arneson's disdain for the self-serving and imperious role the mayor played in the Moscone affair. Emotion bursts forth, however, in the graffiti and caricatures attacking Feinstein on the pedestal of Arneson's bronze self-portrait entitled, with clear reference to recent events, *You Don't Belong Here*.[10] The portrait itself, in the twisting, rending distortion that the artist inflicted on his own head, embodies a troubled internalization of conflict. *Pour Walla* (cat. no. 6), from the same series of bronzes, displays a similar self-directed aggression, although by title and some of its inscriptions it benignly pays respect to Arneson's work at the Walla Walla Foundry in Washington. Such portraits have frequently been compared to the work of eighteenth-century psychotic

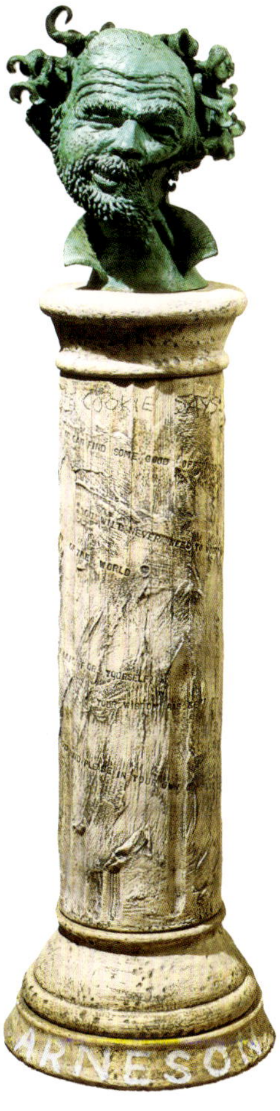

POUR WALLA, 1981-82
Cat. no. 6

sculptor Franz Xavier Messerschmidt, who is known for depictions of his own features in strangely contorted expressions. However, Arneson's emotive self-aggression relates more to the modern sensibility seen in self-portraits by, for example, Picasso and Bacon, where extreme distortion and reconfiguration are signs of the deconstructing of inner psychological states. Donald Kuspit has commented on the self-analysis implicit in Arneson's reworkings of his own bust:

> **H***e shows [the bust's] resistance to fixed shape and place to symbolize its resistance to assigned shape and place. By constantly playing with the relationship between bust and base, and by showing the portrait bust often in wild disarray – the parts of the face as deliberately disequilibrated as the relationship between bust and base – Arneson creates a disruptive, squirming effect, a subtly morbid discomfort that seems a prelude to a metamorphosis of self.* [11]

On 20 December 1981, just thirteen days after the rejection of the Moscone bust, Arneson received a highly unfavorable review in the *New York Times* from Hilton Kramer, a critic who earlier had praised Arneson's "funny" and "brilliant" portrait heads.[12] Writing about the Whitney Museum's exhibition *Ceramic Sculpture: Six Artists*, which surveyed the work of six California ceramic sculptors, Kramer spoke of the general "cultural impoverishment" of the art life of California and, while noting Arneson's technical skills with clay, found his sculptures "provincial" and "dominated by a gruesome combination of bluster, facetiousness and exhibitionism – [that] places a fatal limit on what his gifts allow him to accomplish, or even to conceive."

Always attentive to art criticism, even of the negative variety, Arneson admitted that Kramer's review caused him to rethink his art and its balance of humor and serious moral content.[13] Ultimately, it helped influence a redressing of this balance in the direction of greater moral and political commitment, as manifested in many of his most potent works from 1982 onward. But first, Arneson could not resist a return salvo at Kramer and the attitude of smugness and superiority that pervaded the eastern art historical and critical community. **T**he result was his *California Artist* of 1982-83 (cat. no. 11).

In this funny and defiant self-portrait, Arneson shows the "California artist" as everything that distant observers on the East Coast would expect. Slovenly in appearance, his arms nonchalantly

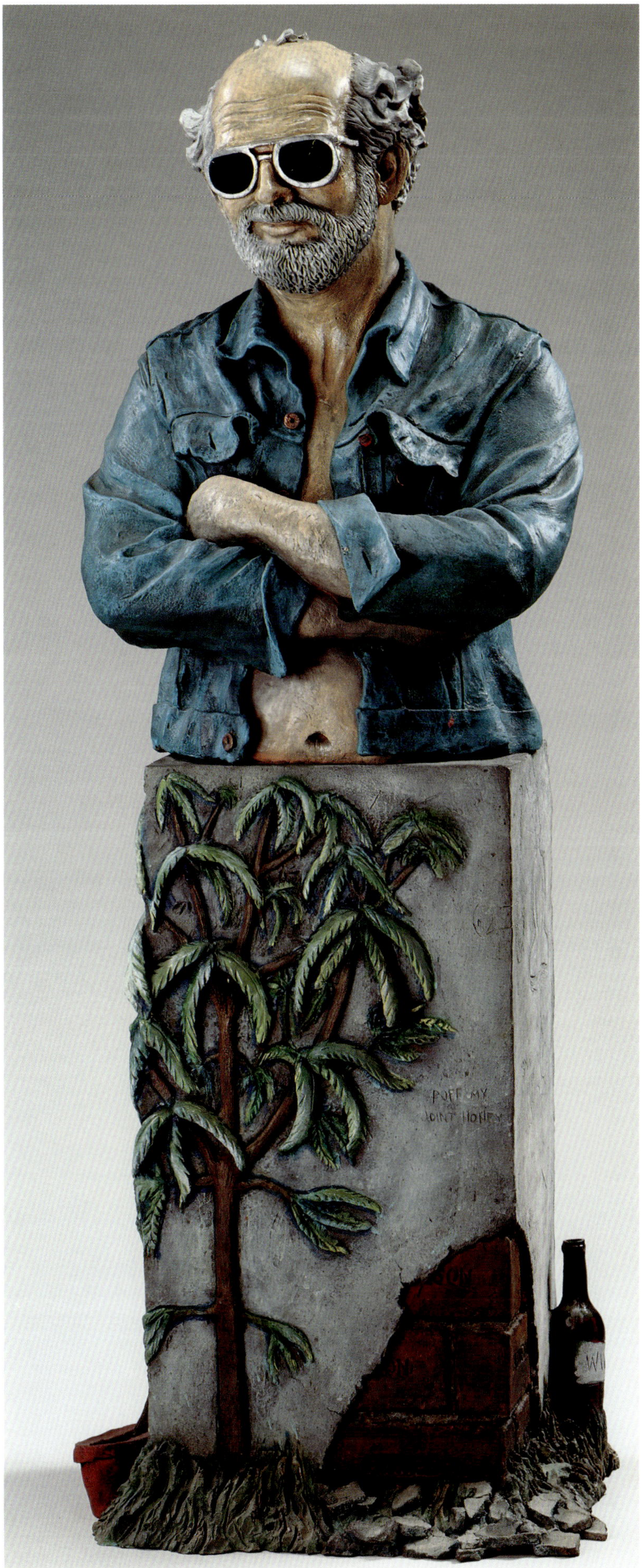

CALIFORNIA ARTIST, 1983
Cat. no. 11

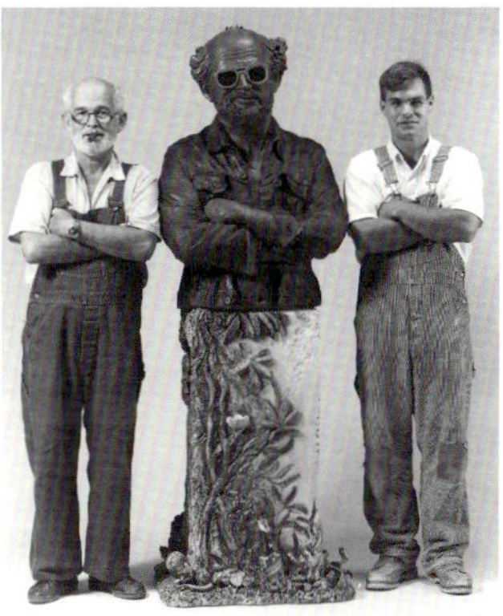

Robert Arneson with
his assistant, George Grant,
and *California Artist*, 1983

folded, Arneson wears a crumpled Levi jacket that hangs open, exposing his bare torso underneath and his protruding stomach. A pair of sunglasses blank out the eyes, which as we see on closer inspection are only sockets opening back into the recesses of an empty head, its interior painted blue to suggest the California sky. The sculpture's pedestal is crumbling at its corner, as if poorly made, with a marijuana plant growing up one side and a beer bottle discarded along the other. It bears an assortment of sophomoric graffiti and caricatures. The sculpture has its sensuous side as well. The bright coloration of the piece, even when seen indoors, seems to capture the brilliance of the California sun, and in both its ceramic and painted bronze versions, its tour-de-force ranges of textures, surface variations, and illusionistic effects are fascinating. Arneson has offered up an iconoclastic gesture that says, "Sure, we're a bunch of slobs . . . So what?" as it refutes through its polemical spirit and genuine inventiveness Kramer's implied charges of shallowness.

From the local political scene of George Moscone, Harvey Milk, and Dianne Feinstein, Arneson soon expanded his subject matter nationally and internationally. Political figures as diverse as Muammar Qaddafi and Ronald Reagan appear in caricatures, both in drawings and sculptures, that react to current events or expose the foibles and failings of leadership. Qaddafi, for example, is seen as a hideous war-crazed monster in a drawing and color lithograph entitled *The Colonel Is At It Again*. The lampooning of Reagan is more tongue-in-cheek. In a group of drawings and two sculptures called *Ronny Portable* (cat. no. 19), not only does the ex-President's face fill a television screen, but his head merges with the box-like shape of the T.V. in a transmutation of the human and mechanical that derides the Great Communicator's packaged-for-T.V. personality. George Bush comes in for harsher treatment. In a drawing entitled *Gulf Dip* and then more vehemently in *Wimp Dip* (cat. no. 27), Bush's grimacing face is drenched in a bath of oil, a reference to what Arneson alleged to be the true motivation for the 1990 Gulf War. A look back at a more distant era is found in *Julius and Ethel with Battery* (cat. no. 21), where Arneson comments morbidly on the execution of the Rosenbergs as a symbol of McCarthyite political hysteria.[14]

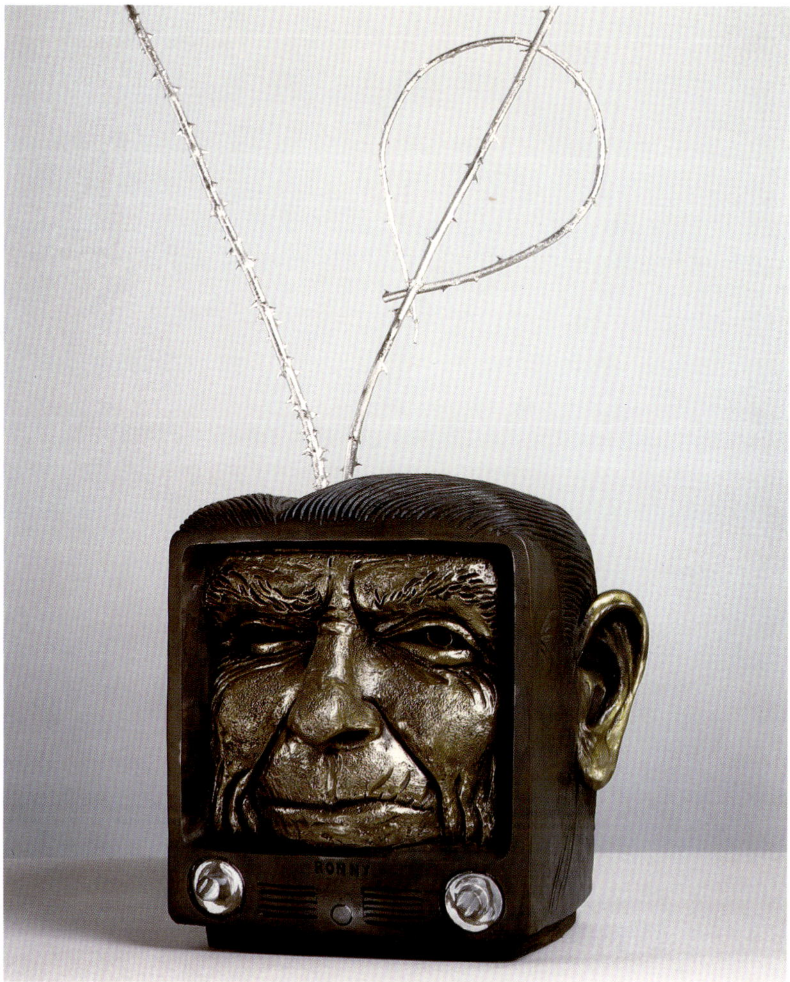

RONNY PORTABLE, 1986
Cat. no. 19
Detail

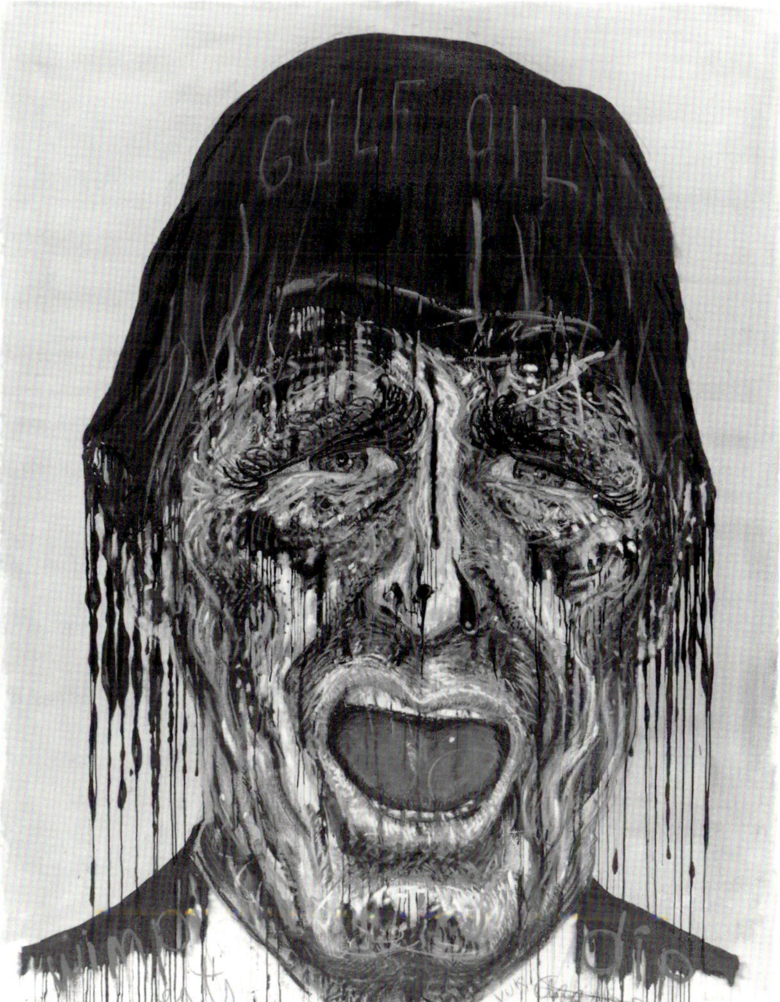

WIMP DIP, 1991
Cat. no. 27

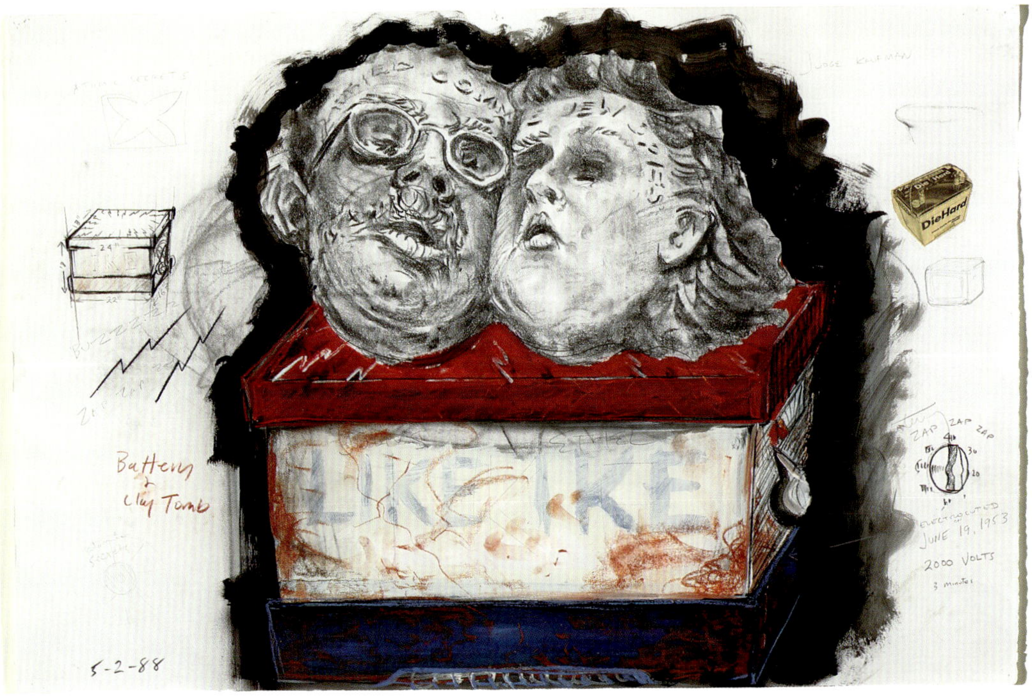

JULIUS AND ETHEL WITH BATTERY, 1988
Cat. no. 21

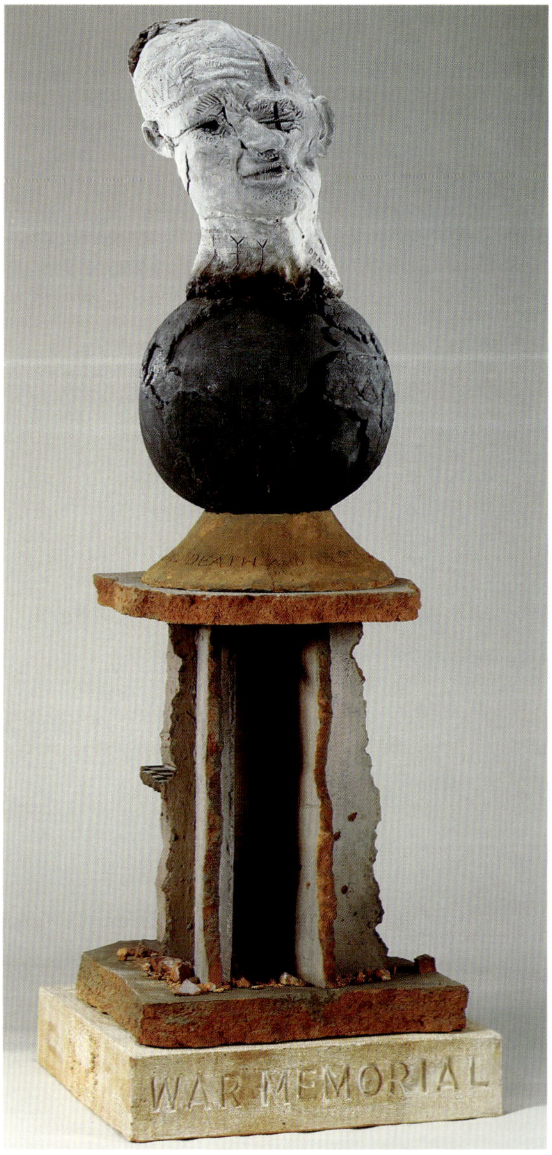

GLOBAL DEATH AND DESTRUCTION, 1982-83
Cat. no. 9

The theme that elicited the most sustained outcry of moral rage from Arneson was that of nuclear war. Starting in 1982-83 with works such as *Holy War Head*,[15] Arneson returned again and again to this subject over a period of several years, creating a twentieth-century Doom's Day Book of images of nuclear holocaust and the obscene mentality of military leaders advocating the use of weapons of mass destruction. His was an emotional appeal, exposing the insanity behind our nuclear arms buildup and attempts to rationalize it through talk of limited strikes and defensive capability. Several works in the current exhibition manifest the intensity of Arneson's exploration of the subject.

Global Death and Destruction of 1982-83 (cat. no. 9) is the earliest work in this group and one of the first in the whole series. As part of a sudden outburst of antiwar sentiment reminiscent of protest art of the sixties, this sculpture and the closely related *Head Mined*[16] and *Holy War Head* redirected Arneson's sculptural thinking from the civic commemoration of *Portrait of George* to war memorials trumpeting the grim prospects of nuclear annihilation. Atop the globe in *Global Death and Destruction* sits a severed head that has been mashed and abused. Sliced cross-hairs over the left eye designate it as a target, and the life that once existed within seems to expire before us. The distressed pedestal, similar to the one in *Head Mined*, invokes the same metaphor of ruin and loss found earlier in Arneson's nostalgic *Fragment of Western Civilization*, 1972,[17] although the agent of destruction here clearly is war and not time.

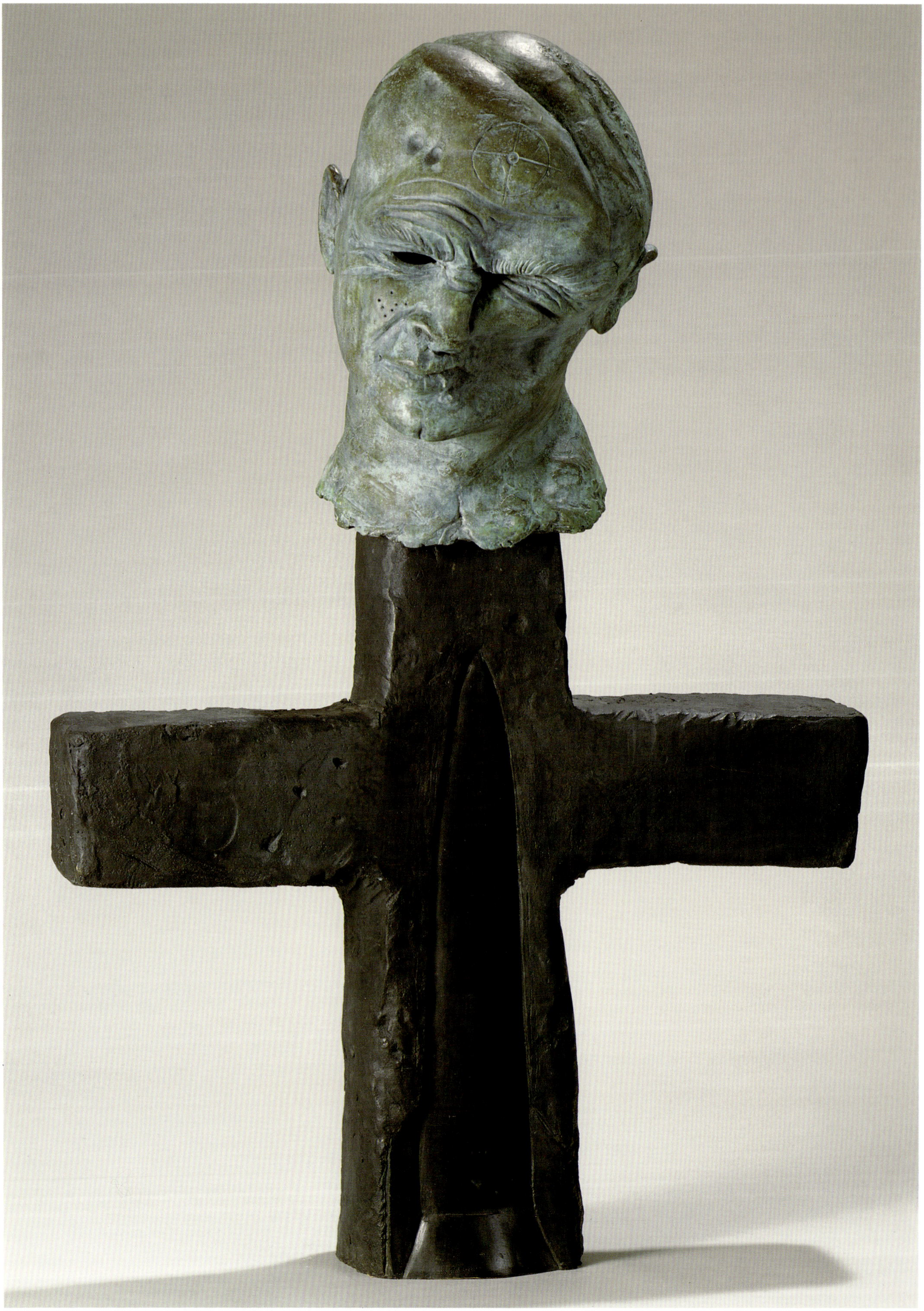

M*inuteman* of 1982 (cat. no. 8) shows a similarly battered head skewered on a cross that bears the imprint of a missile nosecone. Is the message here that religion offers little shield against modern destructive might? Or is the cross a military gravestone, or the mark at the center of a bomb sight? Arneson's calculated double meaning only adds to the evocativeness of this quietly moving work.

Considerably more aggressive in concept are the *Nuke News* of 1983 (cat. no. 13) and *Nuclear Head Kiss* of 1984 (cat. no. 15). Both of these present an incinerated human skull as an emblem of nuclear madness. The bronze sculpture, which clearly pays homage to Picasso's *Death's Head* of 1943, has the rough surface of a cinder and, within its massive, mangled shape, only the vestigial remnants of a human face. Its isolation on the ground without a base gives the head a particularly weighty sculptural presence and a sad remoteness, as the empty eye sockets stare eternally upward. It is a hard, stony, tragic relic, a piece of human debris left as a monument to inhumanity. The various stamped and inscribed markings, such as "Nuclear War Head" and a diagram of an atom, show Arneson's love of graphic notation and wordplay but are gratuitous elements not contributive to the sculpture's strong overall impact.

MINUTEMAN, 1982
Cat. no. 8

This nuclear series derived inspiration from the media coverage of the atrocities in Lebanon as well. The artist was working on a realistic head at the time and found himself distorting it, twisting it, unconsciously working out these events on the head, and in a purely visceral and visual way this impulse kept on generating new work.

Jonathan Fineberg, 1983

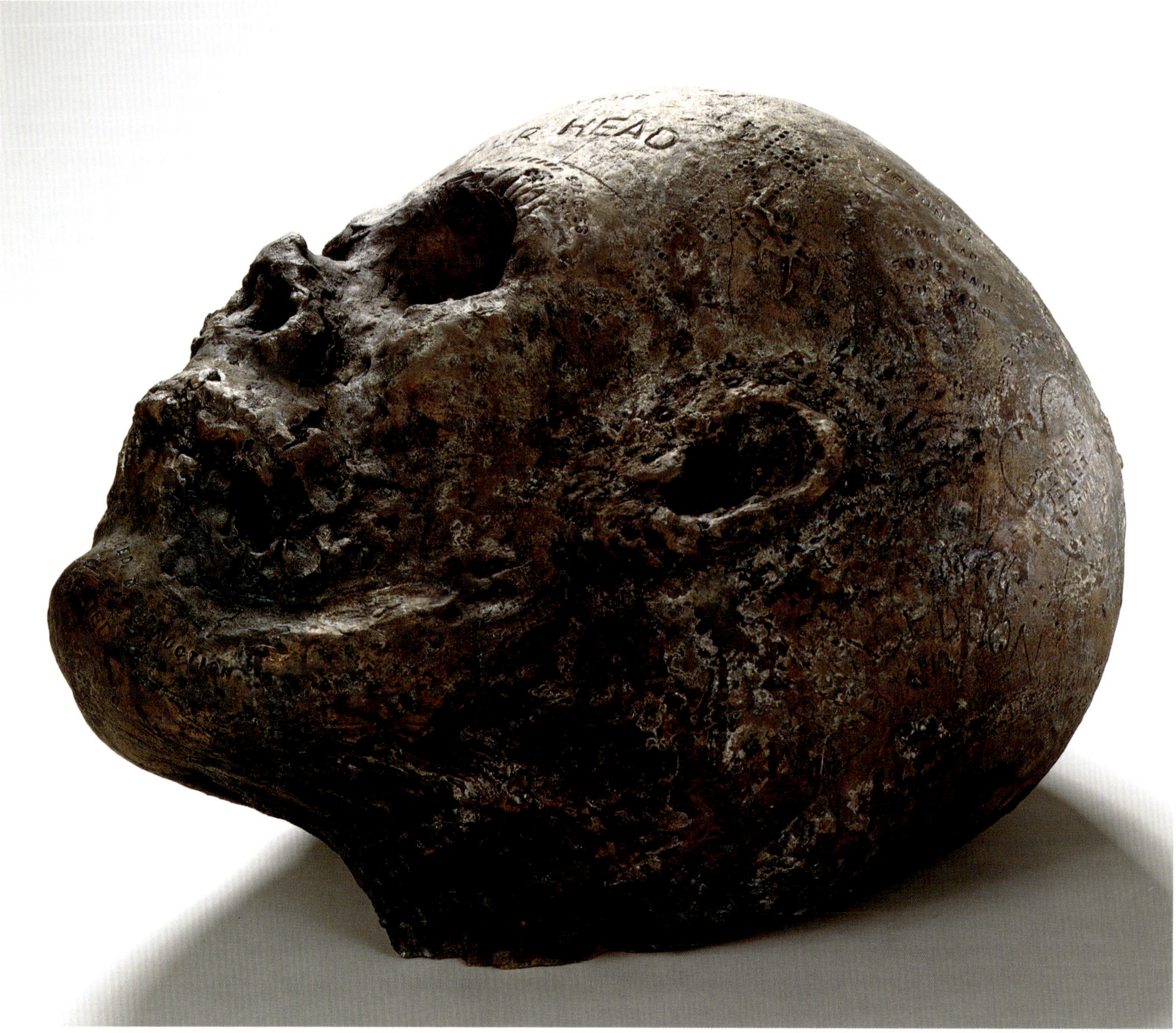

NUKE NEWS, 1983
Cat. no. 13

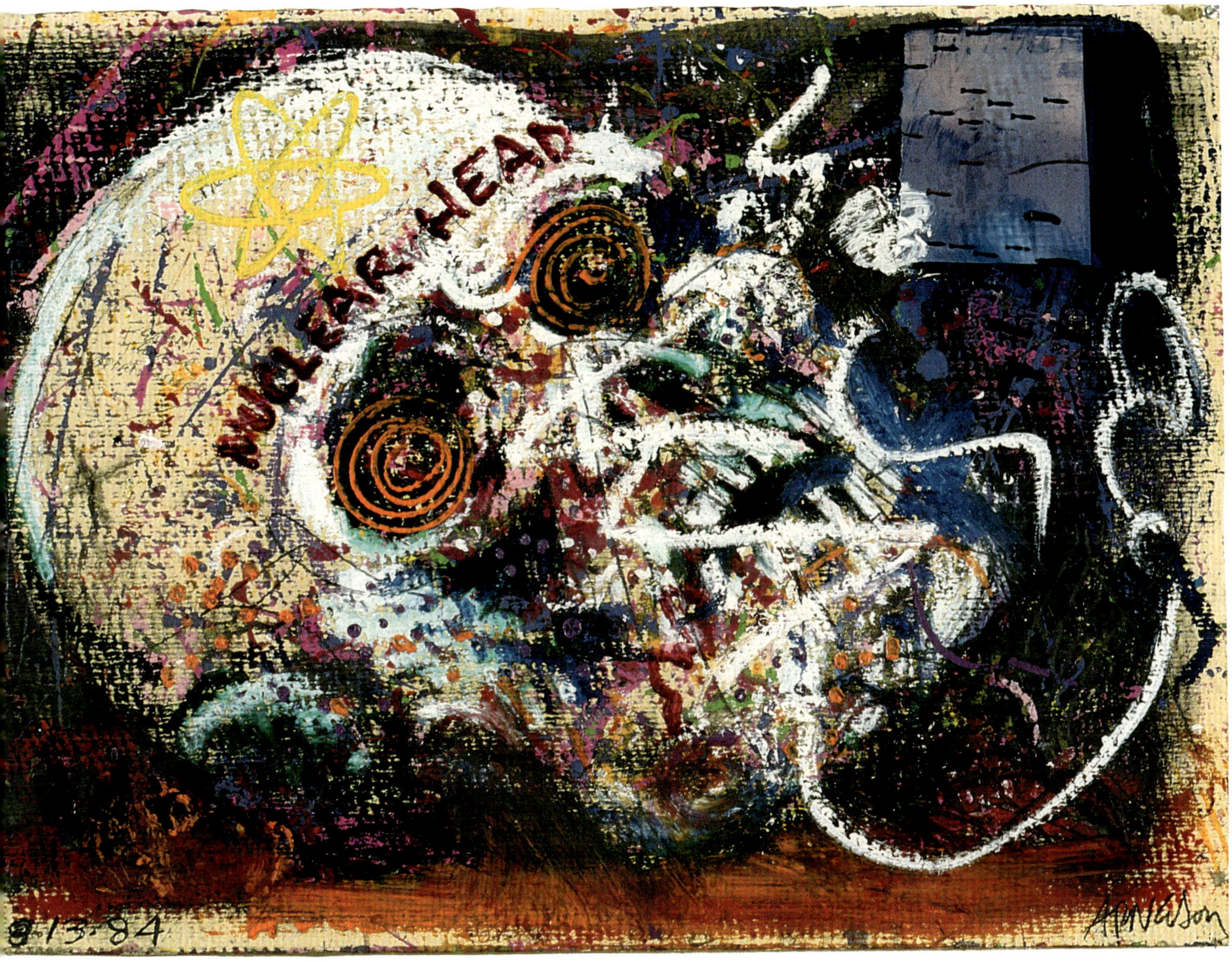

NUCLEAR HEAD KISS, 1984
Cat. no. 15

In the drawing, the skull semi-disintegrates in a welter of strokes, spots, and bursts of color, but still communicates very effectively its memento mori message. It evokes in its wrenching reaction to death the graphics of certain German Expressionist artists such as George Grosz. Content aside, no two other related works reveal better the polar but complementary aspects of Arneson's style: the strong feeling for tactile form in his sculptures and the free, painterly colorism of his drawings.

Why did the nuclear war theme, treated with such singleminded ardor, suddenly become so important for Arneson at this juncture in his career? Its urgency can be attributed in part to international events, such as the heightening of Cold War tensions, the continued failure of international arms negotiations, and, as Jonathan Fineberg has pointed out, recent fighting in Lebanon:

> *This nuclear series derived inspiration from the media coverage of the atrocities in Lebanon as well. The artist was working on a realistic head at the time and found himself distorting it, twisting it, unconsciously working out these events on the head, and in a purely visceral and visual way this impulse kept on generating new work.*[18]

Cognizance of his own mortality, after he had been diagnosed in the mid-seventies as having cancer, undoubtedly contributed to the evolution in Arneson's art of a more expressionist bent, even if he downplayed any connections between his illness and changes in his work.[19] Also important was his growing confidence in his ability to treat harsh themes of broad import in a tougher, more visceral manner, especially in the wake of criticism for frivolity and provincialism.

Of course, Arneson's repetitive essays on nuclear war were not fueled solely by ideological furor. To some degree, there is an echo in these works of the schoolboy making military doodles and caricatures on his notebooks, particularly when they erupt with grotesque humor. *General Nuke*, for example (see cat. no. 14), with his bloody, carnivorous teeth and phallic,

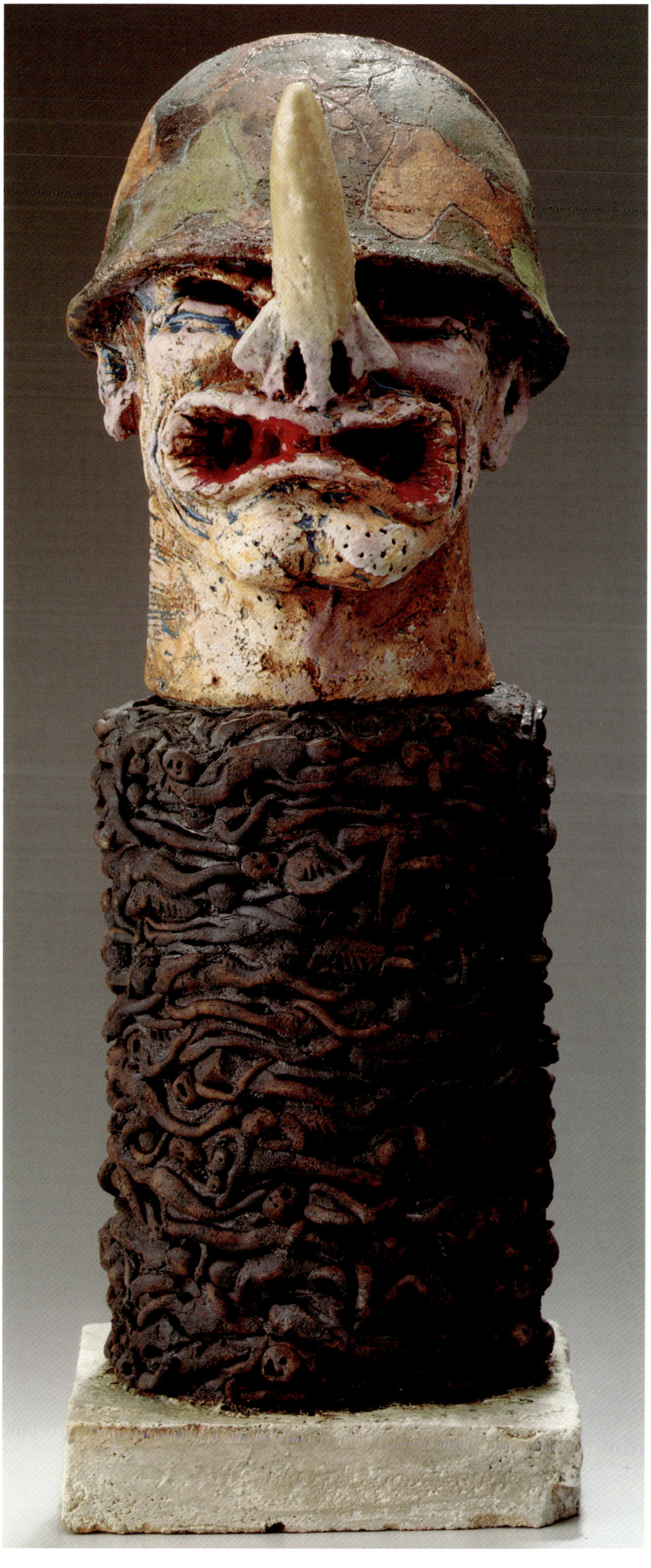

MAQUETTE FOR GENERAL NUKE, 1984
Cat. no. 14

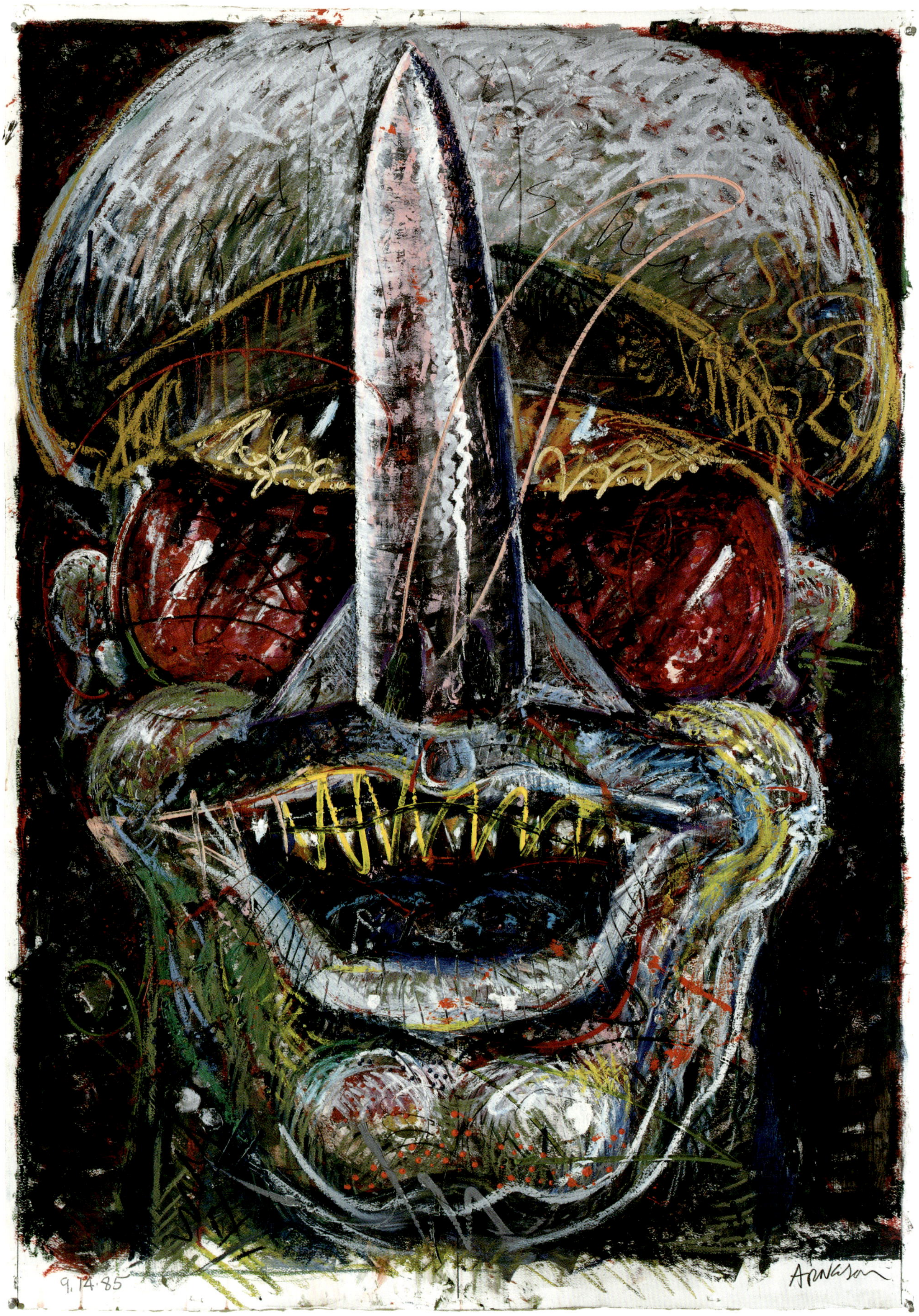

COLONEL HYENA, 1985
Cat. no. 16

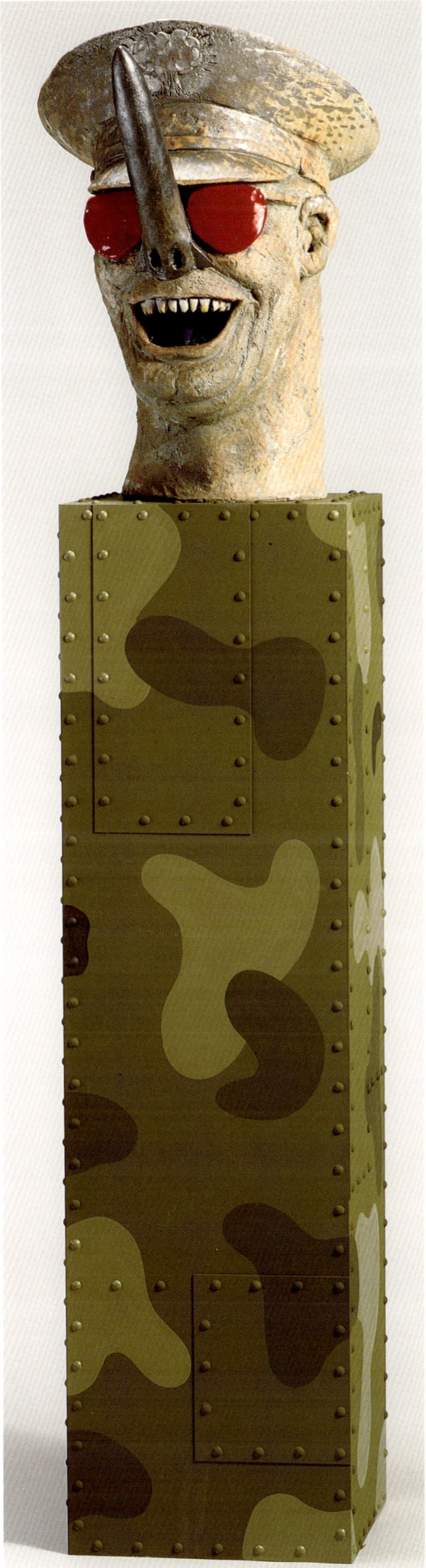

missile-shaped nose that parades his erotic attachment to death, is part monster, part clown, which makes him all the more pathetically dangerous. *Colonel Hyena* (cat. nos. 16 and 17) obviously comes from the same military academy. Departing from his normal use of a ceramic or bronze pedestal, Arneson had a riveted metal base fabricated for *Hyena* and painted it with an Army camouflage pattern.

HYENA, 1985
Cat. no. 17

In his large *Sarcophagus* of 1984-85,[20] the same material is used to form a tomb, over which preside three hideous military officers – a kind of Joint Chiefs of Staff – who are replicated in three independent wall reliefs.[21] Their medals and badges are inscribed with military babble: for example, "Kill a Commie for Mommie" and "Dead Serious – 1st Strike – Son of a Bitch – Guess What? – Apocalypse – Gotcha! – By Kids." More strictly serious is the large drawing *Nuclear Stock Pile* (cat. no. 18), in which a huge pile of dead bodies, recalling tangled masses of anatomy in sculpture by Karl Wiegland, memorializes the human toll of a nuclear strike. Arneson had used the same motif for the base of *General Nuke* and his ceramic sculpture *MXed*. Here, the black, gray, silver, and white coloration, and the loose drawing style combined with a drip technique, consciously invoke the black and white paintings of Jackson Pollock – Arneson even walked on the drawing and left his sole prints, another Pollock reference – although the subject of the drawing concretizes Pollock's abstract language into a grim spectacle of destruction.

Any accusations of shallowness wither in the face of these powerful indictments of the brutality of war. Arneson's visual language is by no means subtle. He has been faulted, in fact, for the excess and overstatement that some see in these works, and a sculpture such as *Sarcophagus* (*fig.* 5) does become indulgent in its superabundance of emotional imagery. But many of his other works hit their thematic target dead-on with a strength that helps both to induce political awareness and responsibility and to capture some of the immensity of human meaning their subjects entail. For examples of other modern sculptures that treat the theme of war as movingly as *Nuke News*, one must go back to Picasso's previously mentioned *Death's Head* of 1934, Alberto Giacometti's *No More Play* of 1933, and Wilhelm Lehmbrück's *Seated Youth* of 1917. *Minuteman* is a solemn tribute to victims of war that achieves on a small scale some of the same expression of communal grief grandly embodied in the Vietnam veteran's memorial in Washington. More caricatured works such as *Hyena* and *General Nuke* give form to the surreal, nightmarish visions of our shared subconscious, visions too extreme for understatement. These and similar sculptures drastically revised public perceptions of Arneson the artist and the person. They have lost little of their power over time.

fig. 5 **SARCOPHAGUS**, 1984-85
Glazed ceramic and painted metal, 80 1/2 x 96 x 30 in.

Shigaraki Ceramic Cultural Park, Japan

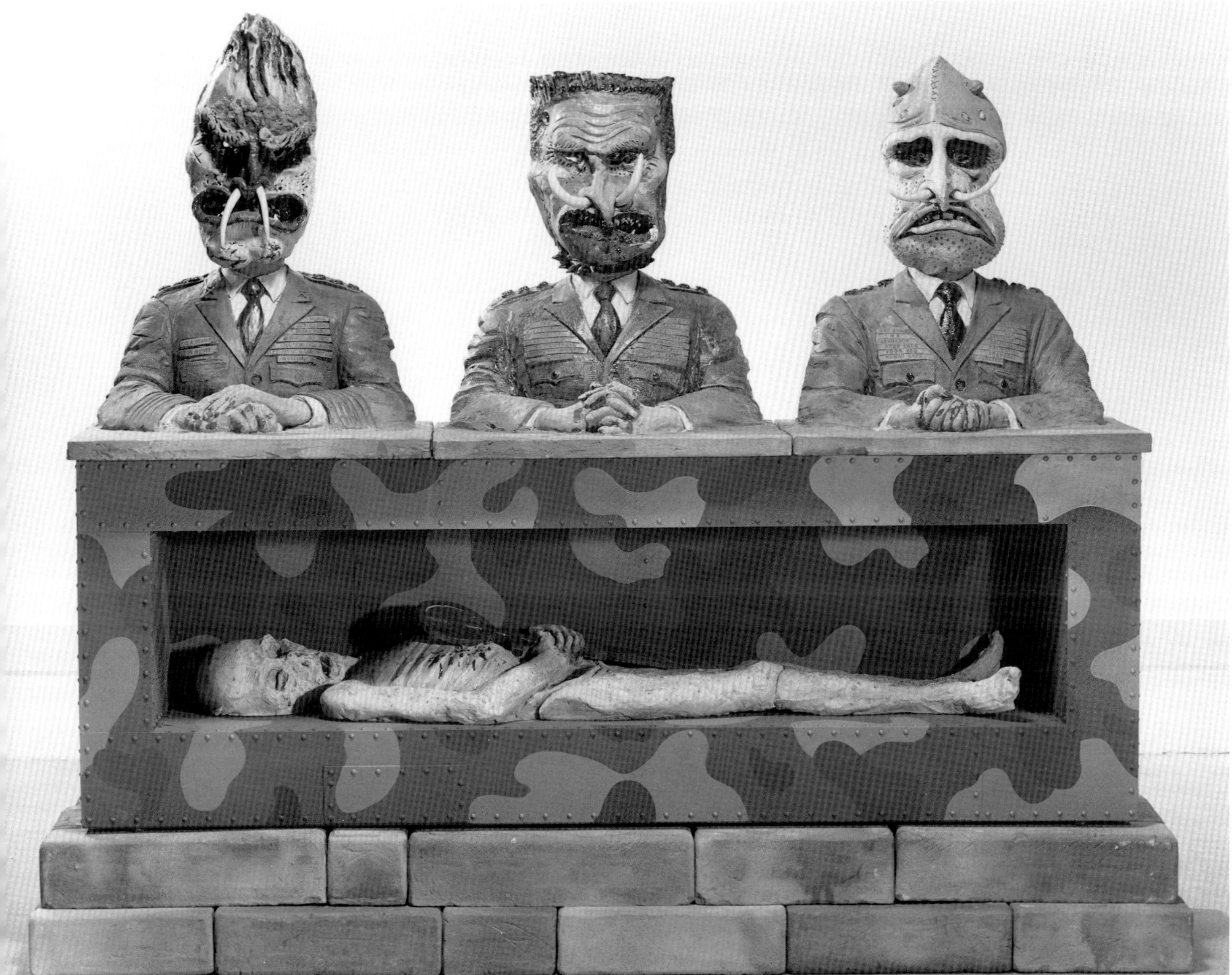

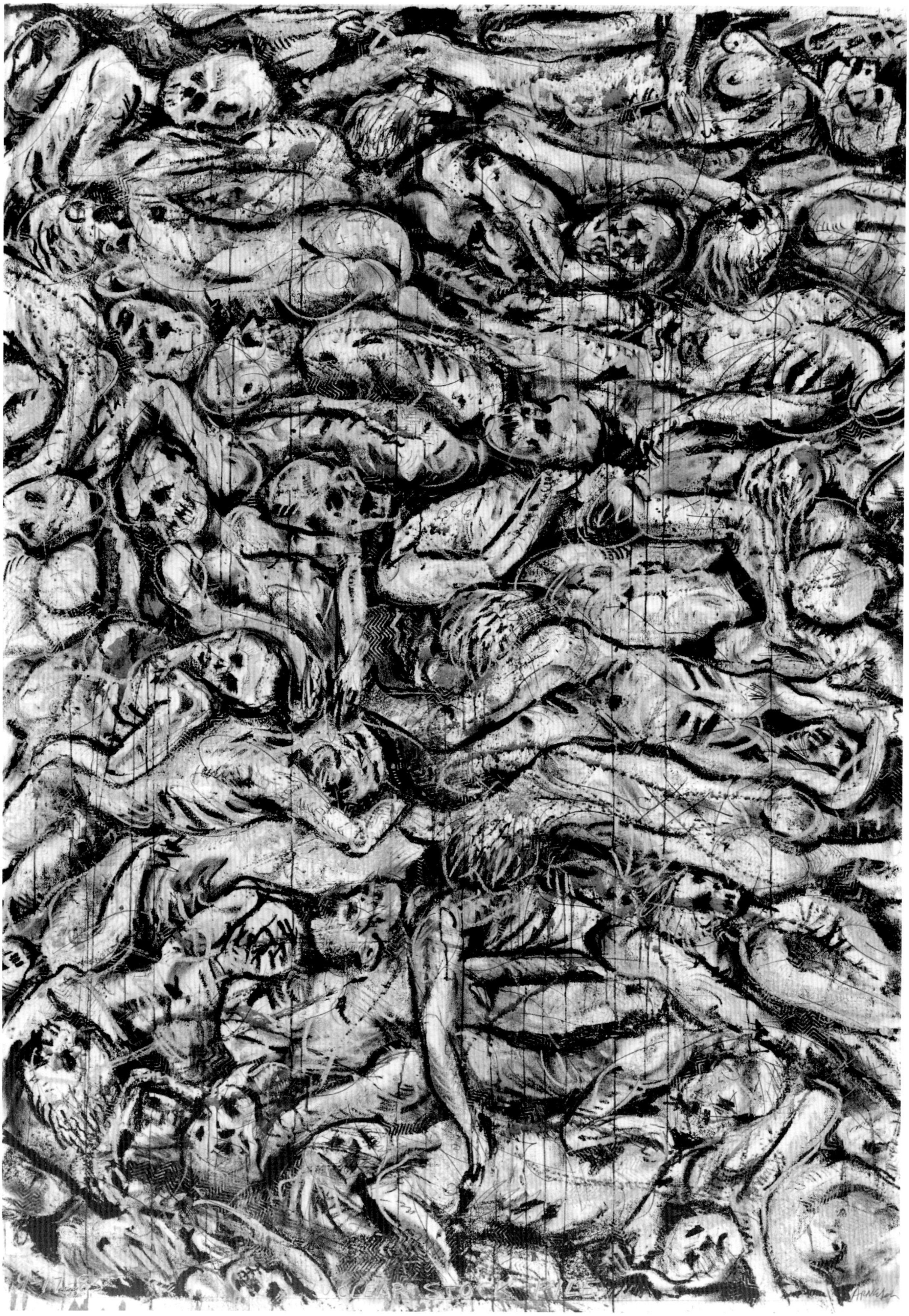

NUCLEAR STOCK PILE, 1985
Cat. no. 18

The deep seriousness of the nuclear series pervades Arneson's other work from the 1980s and manifests itself in themes of more personal, autobiographical import as well as global politics. Lighter moments intervene, but with the *Performance Artist* of 1989 (cat. no. 23), for example, we encounter a sculpture that summarizes with dark, tragicomic intensity many of Arneson's basic attitudes about the role of the modern artist. It is a work that reminds us of one of Daumier's forlorn *saltimbanques*, an earlier symbol of the disenfranchised performer who serves society but is also rejected by it. Arneson's artistic Everyman, another alter ego recalling the Klown of 1978 but less Grand Guignol in concept, wears the white grease paint of a live performance. His head is twisted back in agony and from his nose he bleeds the bright colors of a painter's or ceramicist's palette. Despite the sculpture's initial sensual appeal, its message of inner pain quickly becomes clear. It is a work that tones down the extravagance of Arneson's earlier style to speak in a quieter but perhaps more profound voice.

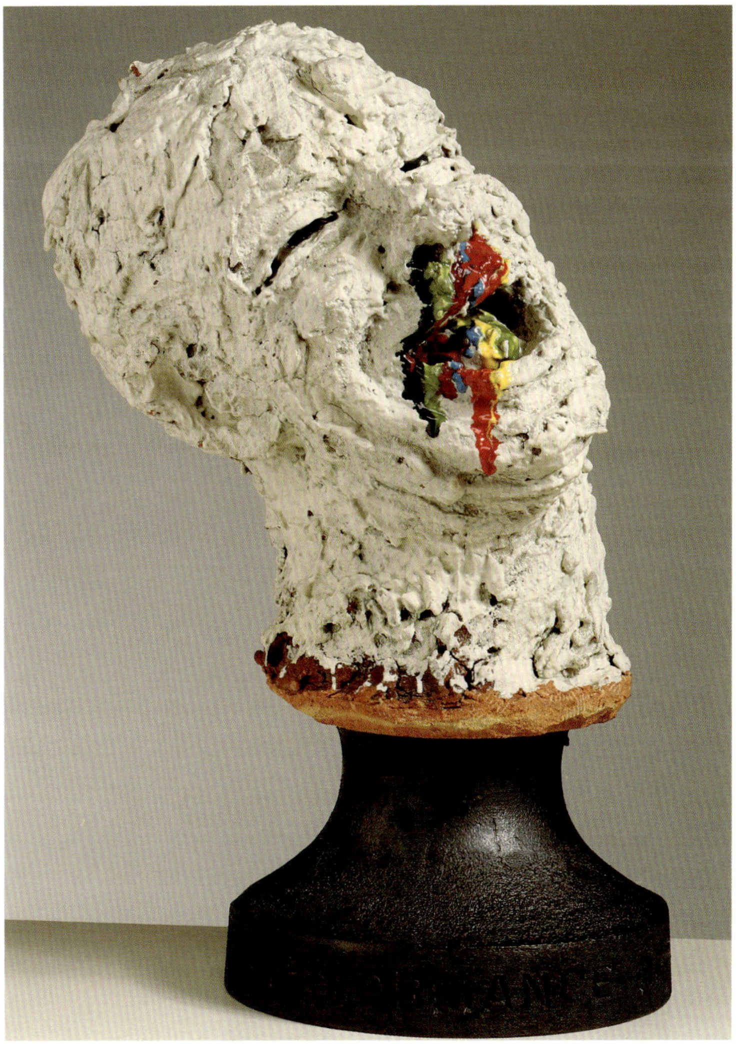

PERFORMANCE ARTIST, 1989
Cat. no. 23

The same interest in the symbolism of the artist underlies one of Arneson's finest achievements, the series of works on the theme of Jackson Pollock. Arneson was fascinated with Pollock the man, the artist, and the icon. He read everything he could find on Pollock and eventually came to feel a close personal identification with this tragic hero of American modernism. The affinity comes through strongly in his work. In drawings and relief busts from 1983, Arneson made the first in a long series of portraits that explore almost compulsively the earlier artist's features, as if by modeling, drawing, and painting him over and over he could understand better the man behind the mask. Often, Pollock's famous drip and spatter technique is emulated in the surface treatment, so that the man and the characteristic skeins of paint become analogous, as they had also in the popular imagination.

Pollock had created a style that revolutionized modern art and became one of its most recognizable avatars. Widely reproduced and imitated, and rewarding to the artist financially, the style came to stand for the man; and as both were popularized and, indeed, mythologized, they were by the same token trivialized. Having experienced himself the dual process of celebration and abuse that art politics can entail, and undoubtedly feeling through his illness a bond with a fellow artist who died tragically young, Arneson not only came to respect Pollock deeply but also found in him a special kindred spirit. He stood for authenticity and individuality in the struggle against societal pressures to conform. As Donald Kuspit has put it, "For Arneson, Pollock's life, like that of van Gogh, was in itself 'political' – both artist's were, in Artaud's phrase, 'suicided by society.' "[22]

J.P.2, 1983
Cat. no. 12

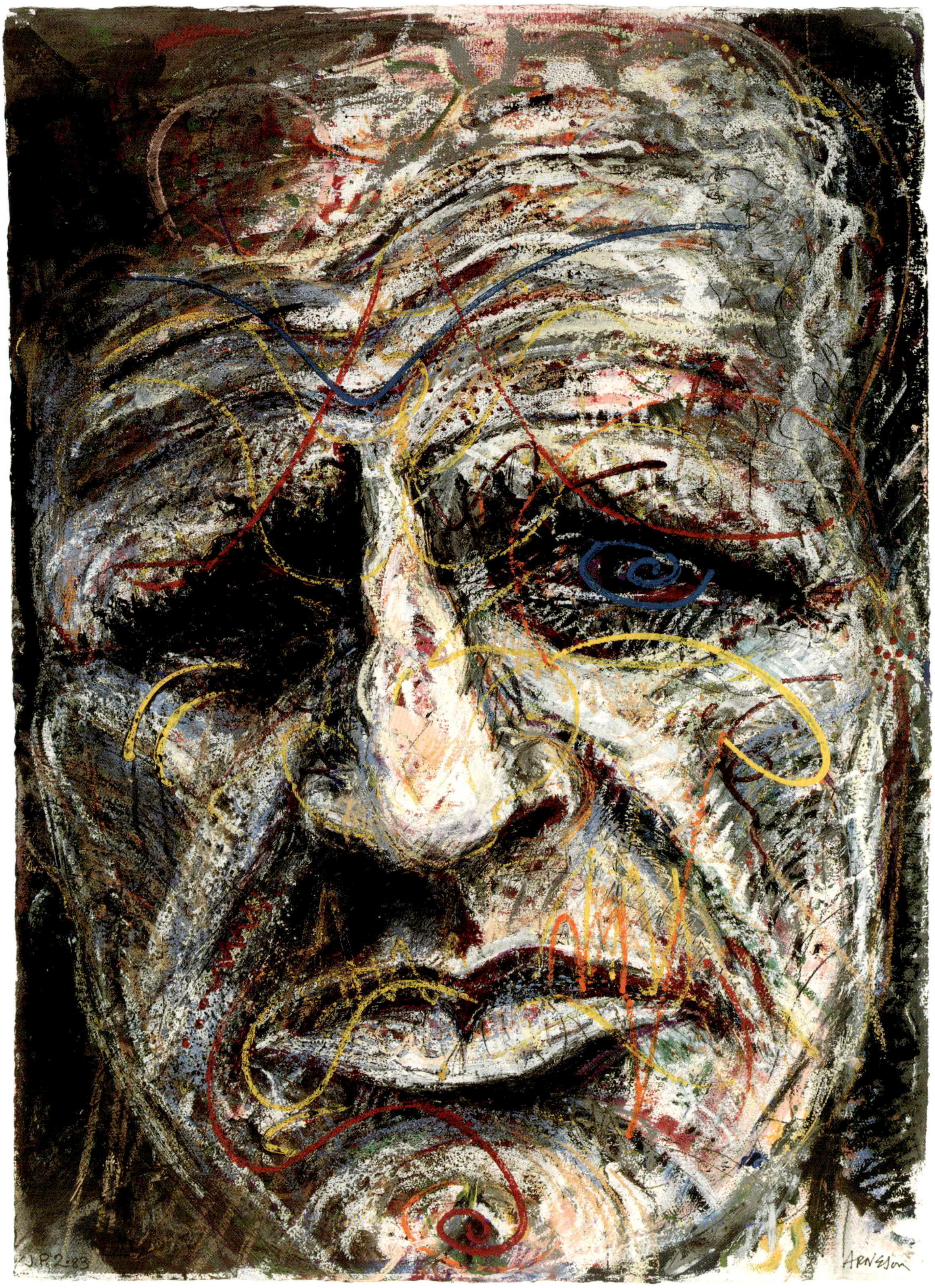

One of the early drawings that best captures this respect is the *J.P. 2* of 1983 (cat. no. 12). This work relates closely in mood and form to the relief portrait of 1983 entitled *Jackson Pollock* and the large drawing *J.P.* from the same year,[23] but it captures with unusual empathy the brooding and distrustful look of the subject. Arneson's portrait busts of Pollock follow on the path of his earlier artist portraits, including sculptures and drawings of Van Gogh, Picasso, Bacon, and Duchamp, that represent personal tributes to these figures, even if somewhat tongue-in-cheek. None of these artists, however, had the same meaning for Arneson that he found in Pollock, nor occupied him over so long a period and through so many works, eventually totaling more than sixty.

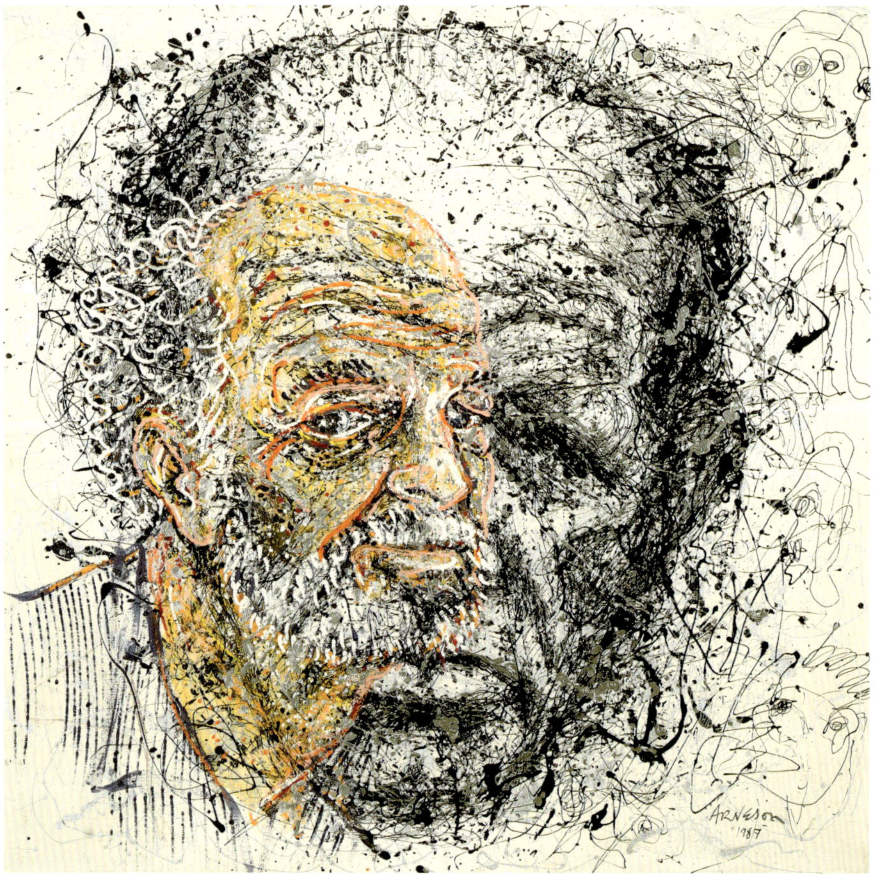

ME AND JACKSON, 1987
Cat. no. 20

No single work states better this extreme degree of personal identification than the *Me and Jackson* of 1987 (cat. no. 20). By imposing his own face over Pollock's, absorbing it into the web of lines and drips that define the latter, and lining up the eyes, he merged visually and spiritually the two identities and channeled himself into the person and the myth that so preoccupied him. Other works pay homage

fig. 6 **GUARDIANS OF THE SECRET II**, 1989-90
Glazed ceramic, wood, Plexiglass, steel, mixed media, 86 x 119 x 26 in.

Estate of the artist

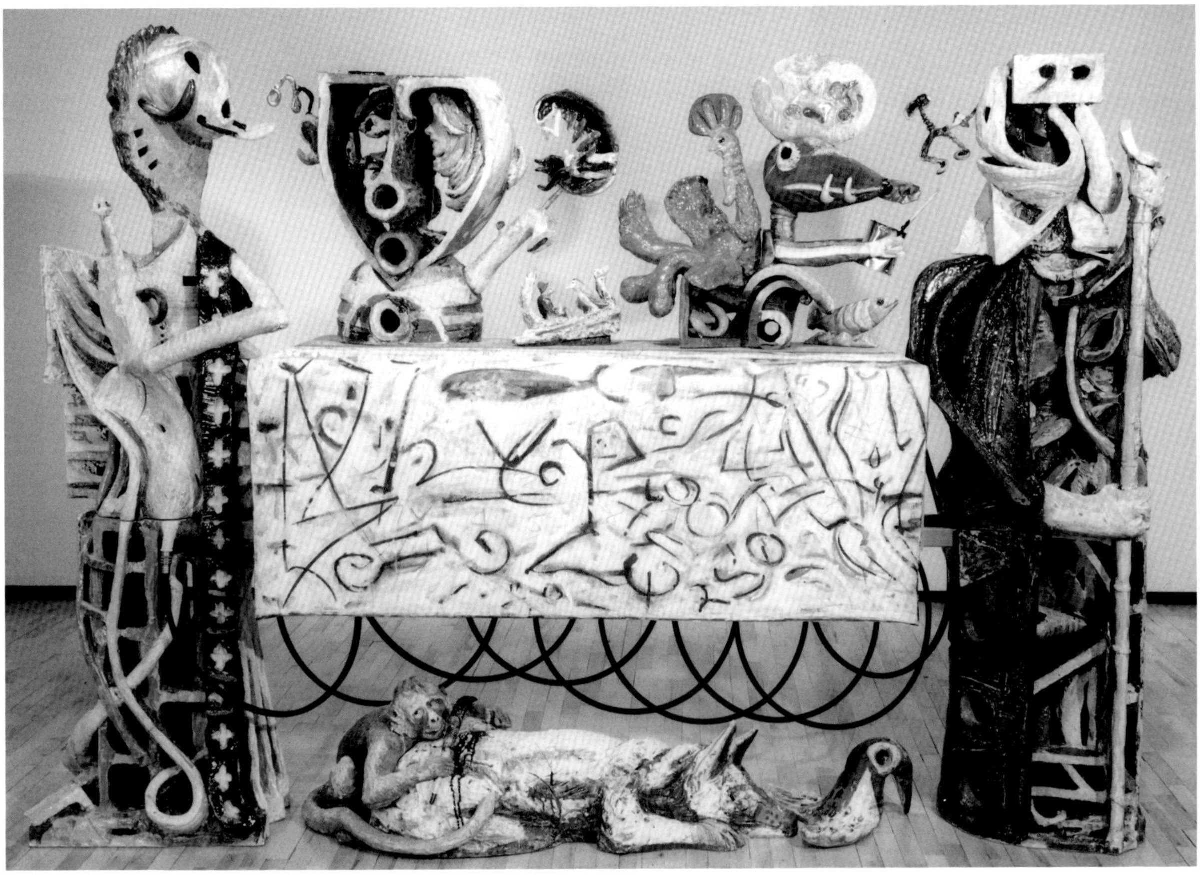

to Pollock in other ways. One sculpture of his shoes, covered with drips and splashes of paint from work in the studio, recalls his earlier *Homage to Philip Guston* of 1980[24] and refers more obliquely to van Gogh's famous painting of old shoes. Sculptured bookends he made of the car crash that took Pollock's life assault in their trivial format the romanticism of the event, while *Cathedral Tower* of 1987,[25] with its classical presentation of a portrait bust on a tall column engulfed in the frenetic, looping strokes of Pollock's famous painting entitled *Cathedral*, introduces an ironic religious note.

Arneson's most ambitious undertaking in this vein was the huge sculpture he made based on Pollock's *Guardians of the Secret* of 1943 (*fig.* 6). This famous painting held special magic for him and perhaps served as an emblematic image of Pollock himself as protector of inner secrets. In another, slightly earlier large-scale sculpture, the wolf/dog from *Guardians of the Secret II* stands atop Pollock's head,

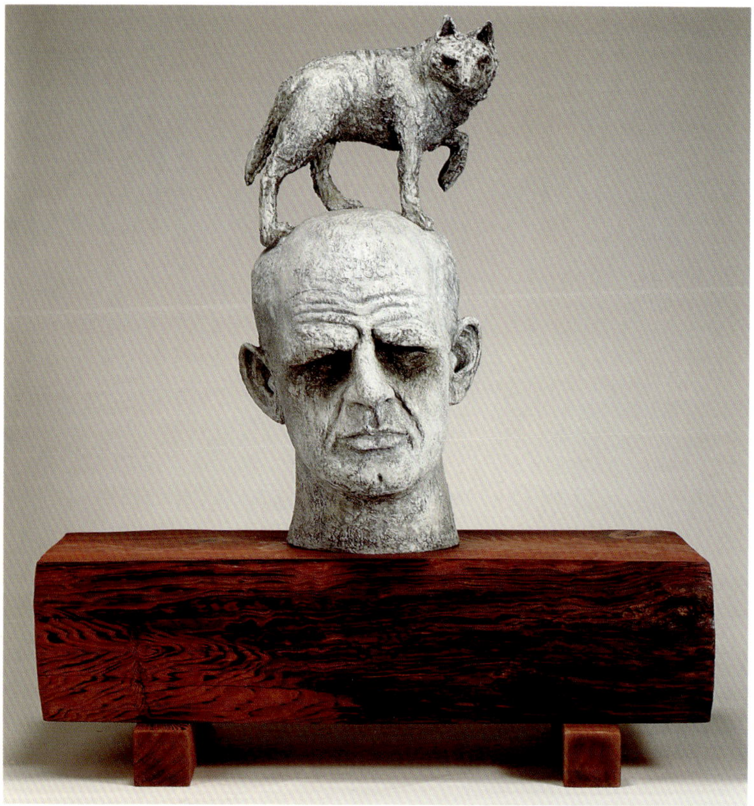

WOLF HEAD, 1989
Cat. no. 22

as a wild, alert, and solitary sentry. *Wolf Head* (cat. no. 22) is one of the consummate works of the entire series. In its quietly sympathetic but haunting portrayal of Pollock the loner and the seer, Arneson created at once a vessel for his own emotion and a masterpiece of modern portraiture.

If there is an underlying sense of fatalism in many of the works considered thus far, it did not diminish the moral responsibility Arneson felt as an artist/activist. He continued until the end of his life to treat social issues. In the small relief sculpture entitled *Gag* that he made in 1991,[26] for example, he shows his own face with a cloth wrapped around his mouth in protest of the increasing weight of government censorship imposed on the artistic community during George Bush's presidency. A series of works on racism from about the same time includes some of his most challenging images. Autobiography again came to figure importantly in his art. While still on the faculty at Davis, he was accused of racism by a colleague and friend, an unfair charge that left him bewildered and wounded. Apparently one of the motivations for the charge was Arneson's repeated and sarcastic use of the phrase "Yas-suh." Ridiculing the misunderstanding involved, he made a large drawing of himself in blackface as a valet or bellboy, with "Yas-suh" inscribed on his cap (cat. no. 26).

YAS-SUH, 1990
Cat. no. 26

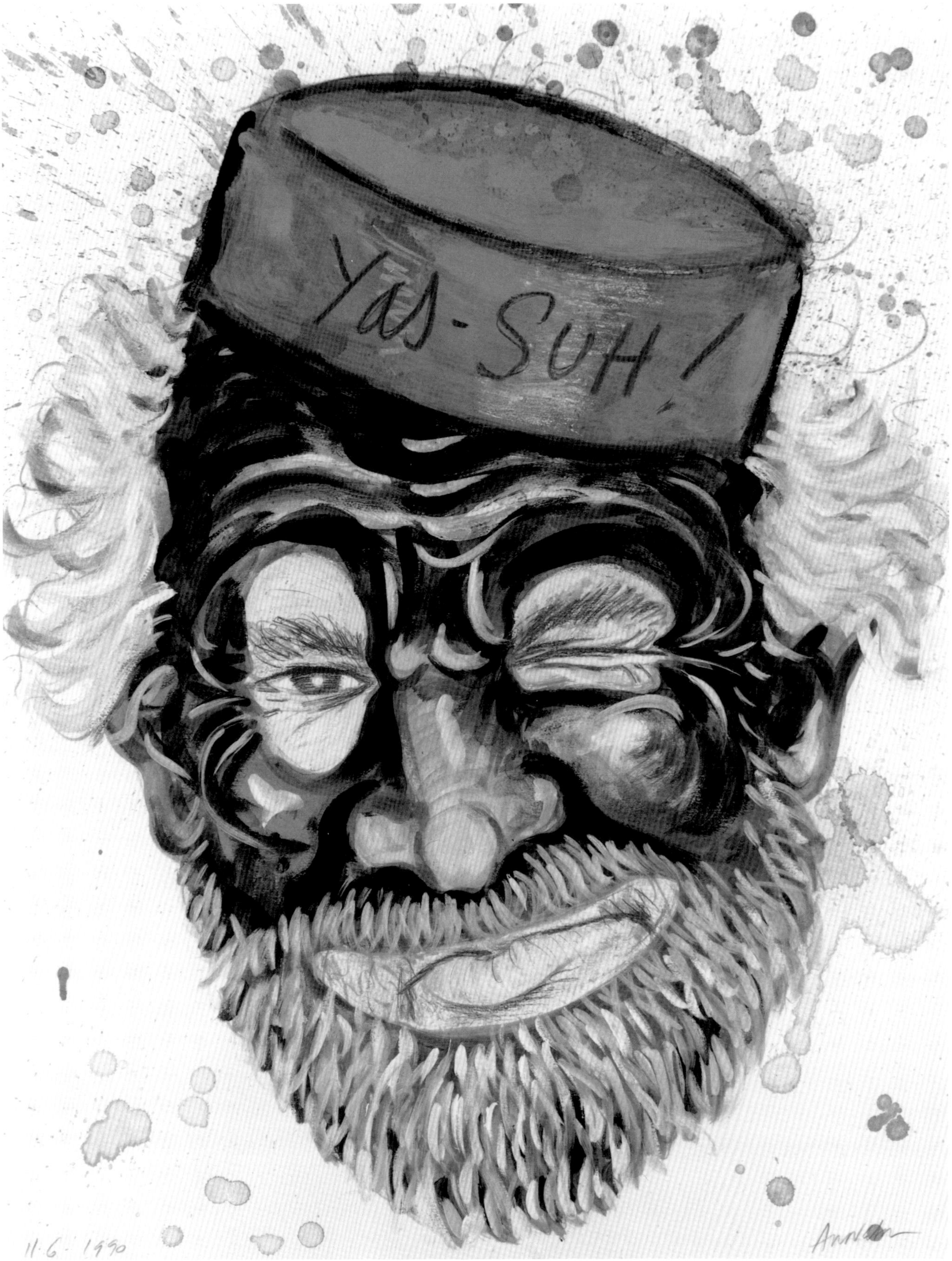

Also reflecting the complicated mixture of guilt and fear that lies within much of the racism felt by whites toward blacks, Arneson painted a startlingly powerful series of portraits of African Americans that confounded his audiences when first shown and remain among his least-known and least-understood works. *By-By Huey P.* and *Yus White and Ugly Man,* both of 1989 (cat. nos. 24 and 25), are representative examples. The former shows the head of Huey P. Newton, one-time leader of the Black Panther movement, who had recently been killed in a drug-related shooting in Oakland. Newton's scowling face, with bloodshot eyes and firmly set jaw, stares out at us in intimidating scale at least ten times greater than life size. Over the face is scrawled in a loose graffiti style a giant praying mantis, an insect that was favored as a symbol especially by the surrealist artists because of its unusual reproductive cycle wherein the female devours the male after fertilization. The reference here may be to the killing off of one's own race.

In *Yus White and Ugly Man,* another grim-looking African American stares confrontationally out of the dark background of a roughly but richly painted canvas. The title leaves little doubt about Arneson's provocational intentions as he explored a white mind-set based on fear and ignorance that stereotypes blacks into a menacing presence. As with the nuclear series, the theme again is violence, but here it is the violence done by one common citizen to another

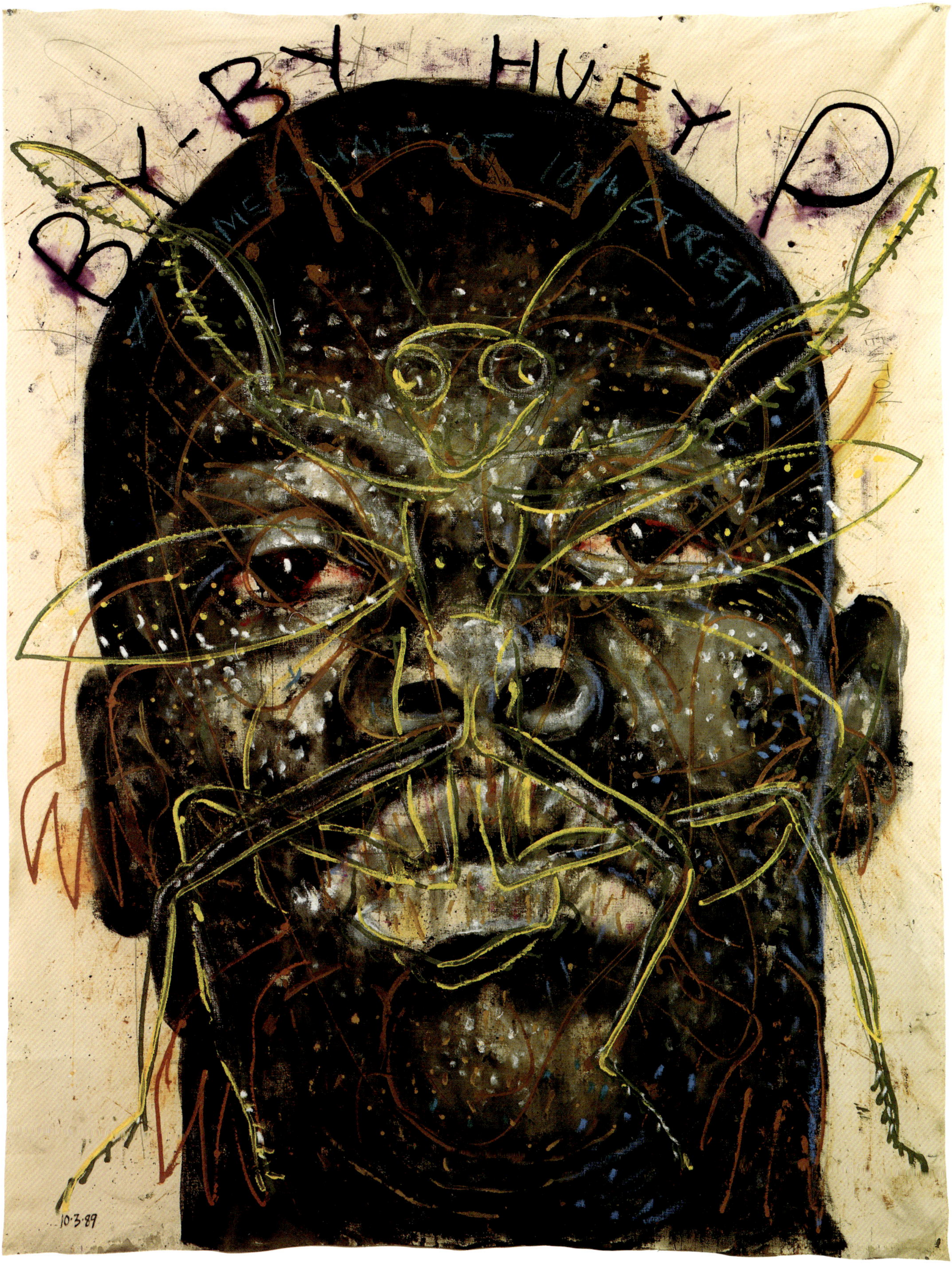

BY-BY HUEY P., 1989
Cat. no. 24

YUS WHITE AND UGLY MAN, 1989

Cat. no. 25

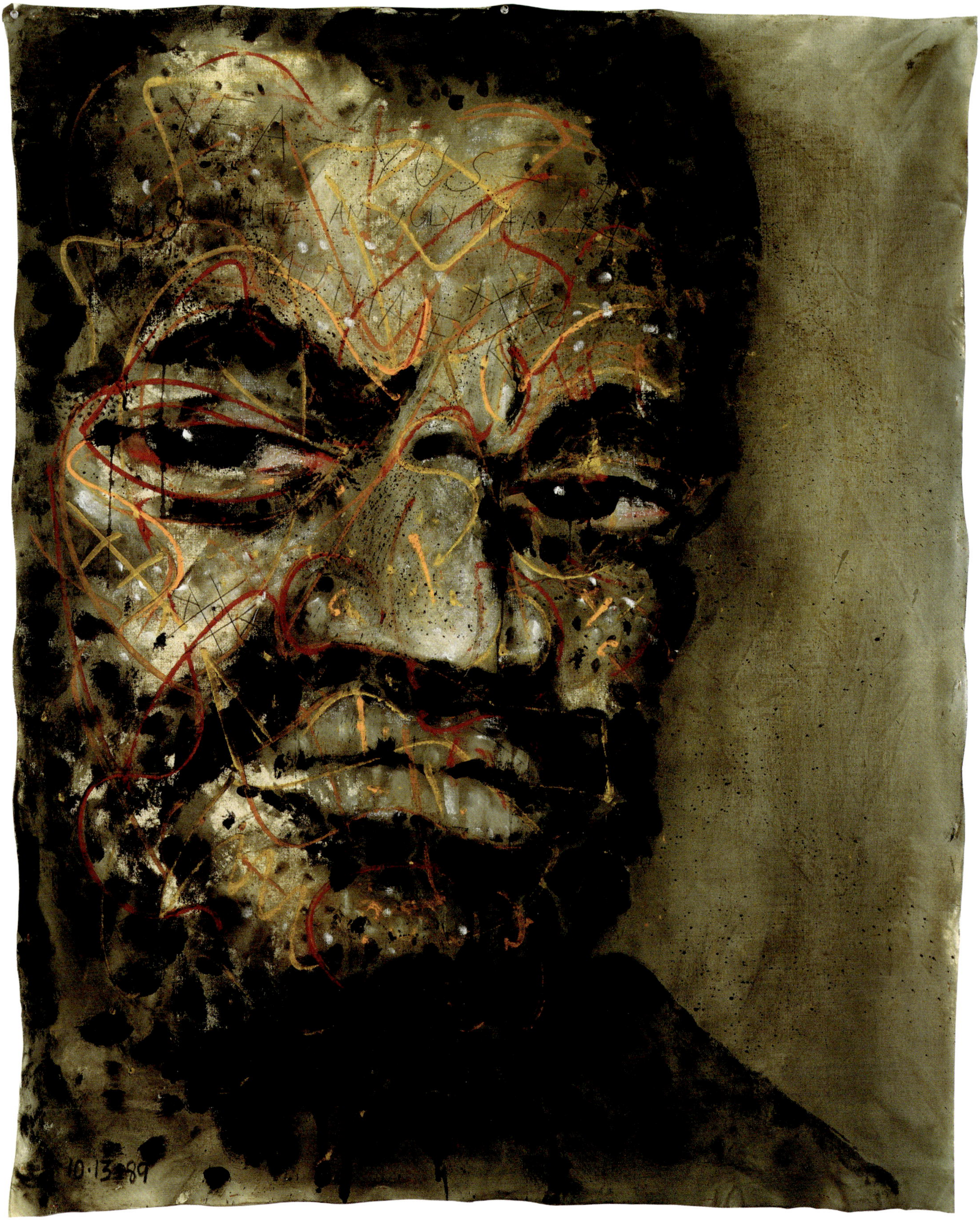

fig. 7 **RAPIST AND DRUG DEALER**, 1989
Glazed ceramic, 25 x 12 x 12 in.

Estate of the artist

fig. 8 **CHIEF EXECUTIVE OFFICER**, 1989
Glazed ceramic, 25 x 12 x 12 in.

Estate of the artist

through mistrust and closemindedness. With more of an ironic twist, the same ideas are conveyed in the two sculptures from 1989 entitled *Rapist and Drug Dealer* and *Chief Executive Officer* (*figs.* 7 and 8).[27] The former is a well-groomed, lily-white male, and the latter is a rough-looking, streetwise black.

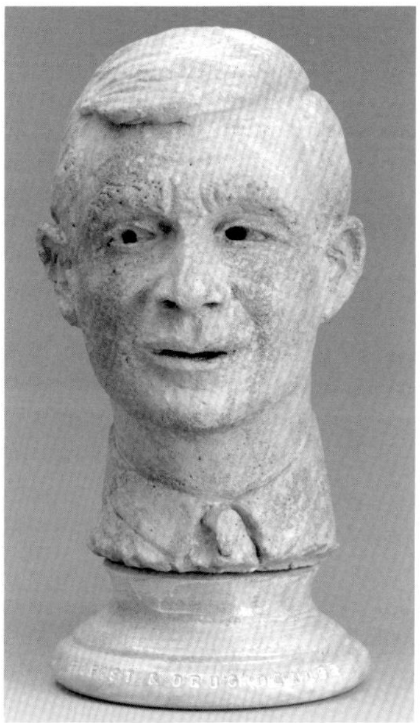

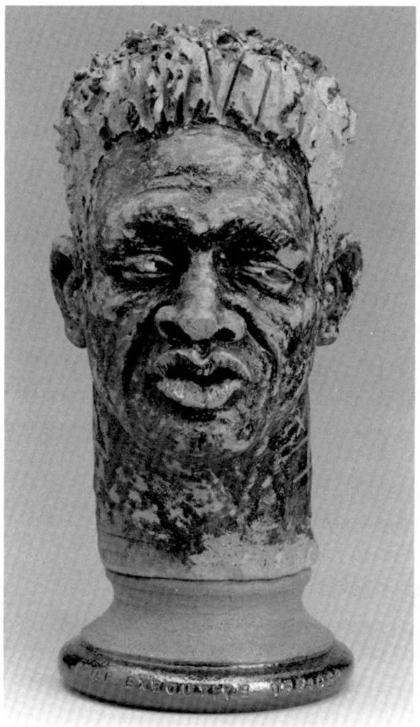

In his typical role of agent provocateur, Arneson invites us in these two sculptures to indulge squeamishly in a note of humor that elides with their distressing seriousness. Humor and politics are two quantities in very short supply in modern sculpture, but Arneson mixes them in a volatile brew that was one of his many weapons for challenging the status quo, questioning convention, and upsetting expectations. In an art world that said "clay is for craft," he based his life on making innovative ceramic sculptures. Against a prevailing trend dictating that the content of art lies in its form, he introduced narrative, symbolism, wordplay, and wit to expand dramatically the range of meaning in his work. In contradistinction to a modernist tradition that had trouble dealing with political and social issues, he made such issues the very basis of his art. Arneson's accomplishments exemplify what Michel Foucault refers to as "the undefined work of freedom," that is, the struggle against strictures placed on free thought and self-definition by the norms of society.

Arneson never gave up the fight.

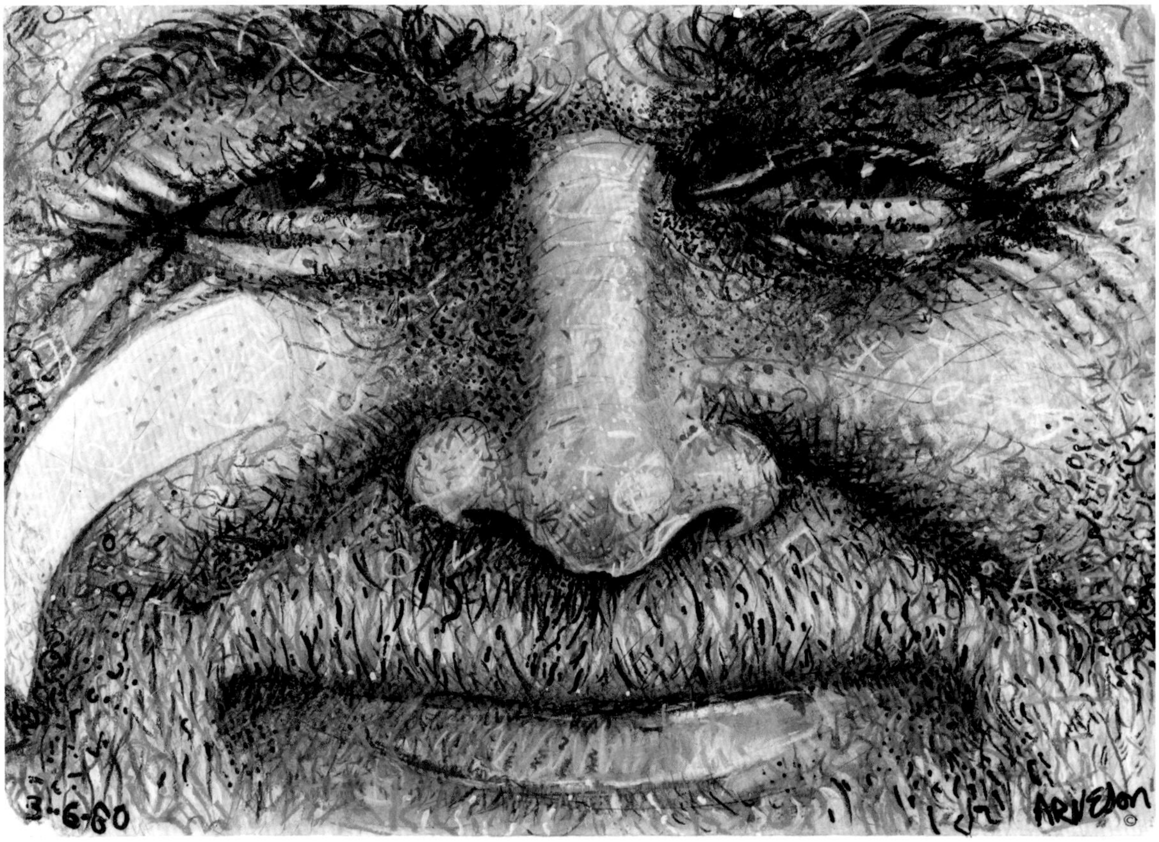

CHEEK, 1980
Cat. no. 1

N*otes*

1. From the Editorial Preface to *possibilities 1*, a journal co-produced by Motherwell and Rosenberg. See Stephanie Terenzio, ed., *The Collected Writings of Robert Motherwell* (New York and Oxford: Oxford University Press, 1992), 46.

2. Arneson's well-known *Klown* from 1978 is a projection of his alter ego as a hapless clown in outlandish garb and makeup, with the inscription "Loko Klown" on its base. See Neal Benezra, *Robert Arneson: A Retrospective*, exh. cat. (Des Moines: Des Moines Art Center, 1986), pl.VIII.

3. Robert Arneson interviewed by Mady Jones, August 1981, p. 59. Roll 3196. Archives of American Art, Smithsonian Institution.

4. Benezra, *Arneson*, fig. 35.

5. Benezra, *Arneson*, fig. 43.

6. Benezra, *Arneson*, fig. 61.

7. For a review of the history of this commission, see Benezra, *Arneson*, 9, 58-63.

8. "In Memoriam, in Storage," *Artnews* 81, no. 2 (February 1982): 13-14.

9. Benezra, *Arneson*, fig. 68.

10. Private collection, San Francisco. *You Don't Belong Here*, together with *Pour Walla* and four other closely related bronze self-portraits on ceramic bases, was exhibited at the Hansen Fuller Goldeen Gallery in San Francisco in April and May 1982.

11. "Robert Arneson's Sense of Self: Squirming in Procrustean Place," *American Craft* 46, no. 5 (October-November 1986): 64.

12. For the earlier comments, see Hilton Kramer, "Sculpture–From Boring to Brilliant," *New York Times* (15 May 1977): sec. 2, 27. Kramer's revised perspective is found in "Ceramic Sculpture and the Taste of California," *New York Times* (20 December 1981): 31, 33.

13. In a conversation with Suzaan Boettger on 28 December 1981, Arneson noted, "Humor is generally considered low art but I think humor is very serious–it points out the fallacies of our existence. Hilton Kramer called me a defiant provincial, and also mentioned moral smugness. Obviously, because I deal a lot with self-criticism in self-portraits, I am going to have to think about all of it." Typescript in the artist's personal papers; quoted by Benezra, *Arneson*, 67.

14. Arneson produced this drawing in connection with a sculpture he made of Julius and Ethel Rosenberg for the exhibition and publication *The Rosenbergs: Collected Visions of Artists and Writers* (New York: Universe Books, 1988). See pl. 32, *2 Fried Commie Jew Spies*.

15. Benezra, *Arneson*, pl. XVI.

16. Benezra, *Arneson*, fig. 76.

17. Benezra, *Arneson*, pl. V.

18. Introduction in Jonathan Fineberg, *Robert Arneson: War Heads and Others*, exh. cat. (New York: Allan Frumkin Gallery, 1983), [10].

19. For observations on this point based on discussions with the artist, see Benezra, *Arneson*, 43.

20. Illustrated in *Robert Arneson*, exh. cat. (San Francisco: Fuller Goldeen Gallery, 1985), 14-15. The related drawing is seen in Benezra, *Arneson*, fig. 81.

21. *Robert Arneson* (Fuller Goldeen Gallery), 10-12.

22. "Arneson's Outrage," *Art in America* 73, no. 5 (May 1985): 136.

23. Benezra, *Arneson*, p. XXIV and fig. 85.

24. Benezra, *Arneson*, p. X.

25. Andrea Miller-Keller, *Robert Arneson/Matrix 110: From the Jackson Pollock Series*, exh. brochure (Hartford: Wadsworth Atheneum, 1990), 3.

26. Illustrated in *Newsletter/Calendar* (Palo Alto, California: Palo Alto Cultural Center, Winter 1993), [1].

27. *Robert Arneson: Black*, exh. cat. (New York: Frumkin/Adams Gallery, 1990), 6-7.

Checklist of the Exhibition

(height precedes width precedes depth in all measurements)

1. **CHEEK**, 1980. *Conté, oil pastel, and oil stick on paper, 30 x 41 in. Inscribed lower left "3.6.80" and lower right "Arneson"*
Achenbach Foundation for Graphic Arts, The Fine Arts Museums of San Francisco, Hamilton-Wells Fund

2. **PORTRAIT OF GEORGE**, 1981. *Glazed ceramic, 94 x 29 x 29 in. Inscribed back of neck "Robert Arneson ©/1981"*
Lent by the Foster Goldstrom Family Collection

3. **GEORGE MOSCONE**, 1981. *Conté, oil pastel, acrylic on paper, 52 1/2 x 42 in. Inscribed lower left "9.1.81/George" and lower right "Arneson"*
Collection of John and Earlene Taylor

4. **VERTICAL GEORGE**, 1981. *Pastels and oil stick on paper, 95 1/2 x 45 in. Inscribed lower right "Arneson/1981"*
Lent by the San Francisco Museum of Modern Art

5. **PORTRAIT OF THE ARTIST AS A CLEVER OLD DOG**, 1981. *Conté, charcoal, collage on paper, 35 x 45 in. Inscribed lower left "8.5.81" and lower right "Arneson"*
Courtesy of Dorothy Goldeen Gallery

6. **POUR WALLA**, 1981-82. *Bronze on ceramic base, 68 x 14 x 14 in. Inscribed back of neck "Arneson 1981"*
Lent by Brian Gross Fine Art, San Francisco

7. **EYE OF THE BEHOLDER**, 1982. *Acrylic, oil pastel, alkyd on paper, 52 x 42 in. Inscribed lower left "9.13.82" and lower right "Arneson"*
Estate of the artist

8. **MINUTEMAN**, 1982. *Bronze, 48 x 31 x 15 in. Inscribed bottom back edge of head "Arneson/1982/AP" and "Walla Walla"*
Collection of Rene di Rosa, Napa

9. **GLOBAL DEATH AND DESTRUCTION**, 1982-83. *Ceramic, 74 1/2 x 26 x 25 in. Inscribed back of neck "Arneson/1982"*
Collection of Ross and Paula Turk

10. **HARVEY MILK**, 1983. *Conté, acrylic, oil stick on paper, 41 x 30 in. Inscribed lower right "Arneson '83"*
Courtesy of John Berggruen Gallery

11. **CALIFORNIA ARTIST**, 1982, *bronze cast 1983. Painted bronze, 78 x 29 x 23 1/2 in. Inscribed lower back edge of bust "Arneson" and "© Walla Walla /AP"*
Courtesy of John Berggruen Gallery

12. **J.P.2**, 1983. *Oil and acrylic on paper, 41 x 30 in. Inscribed lower left "J.P.2. 83" and lower right "Arneson"*
Collection of Patricia Bransten

13. **NUKE NEWS**, 1983. *Bronze, 26 x 22 x 19 in. Inscribed under chin "Arneson 1983" and back edge underneath "© 1/3/1983 Walla Walla"*
Collection of The Runnymede Sculpture Farm, founded by John and Dodie Rosekrans

14. **MAQUETTE FOR GENERAL NUKE**, 1984. *Glazed ceramic, 17 x 6 x 8 1/2 in.*
Estate of the artist

15. **NUCLEAR HEAD KISS**, 1984. *Oil, acrylic, collage on paper, 13 1/2 x 31 3/4 in. Inscribed lower left "8.13.84" and lower right "Arneson"*
Courtesy of Frumkin/Adams Gallery

16. **COLONEL HYENA**, 1985. *Mixed media on paper, 53 x 37 in. Inscribed lower left "9.14.85" and lower right "Arneson"*
Collection of Ross and Paula Turk

17. **HYENA**, 1985. *Glazed ceramic on painted metal base, 75 1/2 x 17 x 24 in.*
Collection of Claire E. Flagg

18. **NUCLEAR STOCK PILE**, 1985. *Mixed media on paper, 80 1/2 x 58 1/2 in. Inscribed lower left "9.17.85" and lower middle "Nuclear Stock Pile" and lower right "Ar*
Lent by Brian Gross Fine Art, San Francisco

19. **RONNY PORTABLE**, 1986. *Bronze, 35 1/2 x 21 1/2 x 14 in. Inscribed on back at bottom "Arneson 1986" and "Walla Walla © 1986 2/3"*
Courtesy of Dorothy Goldeen Gallery

20. **ME AND JACKSON**, 1987. *Enamel and oil on canvas, 58 3/4 x 58 3/4 in. Inscribed lower right "Arneson/1987"*
Collection of Barbara and Gerson Bakar

21. **JULIUS AND ETHEL WITH BATTERY**, 1988. *Mixed media on paper, 30 1/4 x 44 1/2 in. Inscribed lower left "5.2.88" and lower right "Arneson"*
Courtesy of Riva Yares Gallery

22. **WOLF HEAD**, 1989. *Bronze on redwood base, 83 x 73 x 36 in. Inscribed back of head "Arneson 1989"*
Estate of the artist

23. **PERFORMANCE ARTIST**, 1989. *Glazed ceramic, 28 1/2 x 16 x 17 in. Inscribed lower back edge "Arneson '89"*
Courtesy of John Berggruen Gallery

24. **BY-BY HUEY P.**, 1989. *Latex, acrylic, oil stick on canvas, 77 x 58 in. Inscribed lower left "10.3.89" and lower right "Arneson"*
Courtesy of Frumkin/Adams Gallery

25. **YUS WHITE AND UGLY MAN**, 1989. *Acrylic on canvas, 58 x 46 in. Inscribed lower left "10.13.89"*
Estate of the artist

26. **YAS-SUH**, 1990. *Mixed media over lithograph, 36 3/4 x 28 in. Inscribed lower left "11.6.1990" and lower right "Arneson"*
Estate of the artist

27. **WIMP DIP**, 1991. *Pastel, acrylic, oil stick, plastic enamel on canvas, 94 1/2 x 72 in. Inscribed lower left "2.20.91" and lower right "Arneson"*
Courtesy of John Natsoulas Gallery

Chronology
by Mary Maggini

930 September 4. Born in Benicia, California, to Arthur and Helena Arneson. Robert is their second son; he has an eight-year-old brother, Vernon.

933-45 Arneson's father, an accomplished draftsman, teaches him to draw at age three or four. Over the next ten years, Arneson develops an interest in drawing comics.

948 Although his cousin attends California College of Arts and Crafts (CCAC) in Oakland and urges him to enroll, Arneson is more interested in sports and attends the College of Marin. While at Marin he becomes sports editor of the college paper Mariner and supplies cartoons. Receives a "D" in an introductory ceramics class. Graduates from College of Marin, January, 1951.

950 Encouraged by teachers to continue studying art, he receives a partial scholarship to CCAC where he takes commercial art courses. Drops out for a year to work at the Shell Refinery. Re-enrolls at CCAC for two and one-half years, and is a moderately successful watercolorist. Awarded degree in Art Education.

953-54 Begins teaching art at Menlo-Atherton High School (until 1957) and practices ceramics at night. Attends summer school at San Jose State and studies ceramics with Herbert Saunders. Begins reading Ceramics Monthly; follows Carlton Ball's column faithfully and tries out Ball's suggestions on his high school art classes.

955 Marries Jeannette Jensen. Over the years they will have four sons: Leif, Kreg, Derek, and Kirk.

956 Returns to CCAC to study ceramics with Edith Heath. Some students leave to work with the more avant-garde ceramic sculptor Peter Voulkos, then teaching in Los Angeles.

957 Abandons other forms of art and pursues ceramics. Enters a graduate program at Mills College in Oakland to study with Antonio Prieto. Exposed to the work of Peter Voulkos and begins to do sculptural ceramics under his influence.

958 Graduates from Mills with an M.F.A. and is offered a position at Santa Rosa Junior College teaching ceramics, teacher education, and design. Begins doing pottery demonstrations at the California State Fair in Sacramento; makes wine bottles to sell at Gump's.

959 Meets Voulkos for the first time. Is offered a job at Central Washington College of Education in Washington State, which he turns down to stay in the Bay Area; gets a job at Fremont High School teaching art for one year.

960 Teaches art at Mills College for the next two years. Incorporates more of an Abstract Expressionist idiom in his ceramics. Begins having problems with Prieto over progressive interests. First show at The Oakland Museum: two-man show with Tony Delap. Work develops into what he terms his "organic, quasi-Voulkos" period.

961 At the California State Fair Ceramics Booth, Arneson makes No Deposit, No Return, the earliest of his deadpan Pop Art objects, and begins, as a joke, to make dinner plates holding clay food. Meets Wayne Thiebaud and Mel Ramos, who also work at the fair.

962 First San Francisco museum show at the de Young Museum: Robert Arneson: Ceramics, Drawings, and Collages. Simultaneously, Wayne Thiebaud is showing paintings of hamburgers and pies at the de Young. Appointed Assistant Professor of Art and Design at University of California, Davis, and hired by the College of Agriculture to teach design. Teaches in TB9 (temporary building 9), erected in 1928. Also housed in the building are the police department, dairy storage, the mail department, the headquarters for food service, and a bronze foundry. Over the years, Arneson's ceramics department slowly takes over the entire facility.

963 Chosen as one of the artists to exhibit in the show California Sculpture at the Kaiser Center Roof Garden, curated by John Coplans, then editor of Artforum. Also included in the show are Ed Kienholz, Simon Rodia, Manuel Neri, John Mason, and Voulkos, among others. This is a pivotal exhibition for Arneson in the establishment of his own stylistic identity. Exploiting the most fundamental and mundane of ceramic traditions, he creates a toilet of stoneware. Believes he has finally made "a Bob Arneson." Installed on a pedestal at Kaiser Center, it is immediately attacked by a vice president at the company and removed by Coplans. Sells the work to a friend, whose husband intentionally breaks it.

1964 Shows with Allan Stone in New York for the first time. Also begins to sell work regularly at the Candy Store Gallery in Folsom, owned by Adeliza McHugh. This provides Arneson's first regular income from art: for one year, $100 per month.

1966 Shows again with Allan Stone. The exhibition consists of Pop images, including Typewriter and Toaster. The former is incorporated in Dada, Surrealism, and Their Heritage, shown at the Museum of Modern Art in New York in 1968. Arneson shows at U.C. Davis with his students, including David Gilhooly, Richard Shaw, Jim Adamson, Margaret Dodd, Bruce Nauman, Chris Unteseher, and Jerry Walburg. Show receives favorable notices, except for Arneson's work, which consists of large colored roses. Intrigued with color, Arneson has urged his students to approach ceramics as a painting process. He begins using white, low-fire clay, which allows the imposition of bright color onto the work. Begins Alice Street series, based on a tract home he and Jeannette had bought in Davis at the corner of Alice and L Streets. He makes "house sketches": small (ten-inch) houses in clay. As the scale of the works grows, he develops a modular system of building, and incorporates the imagery into cups, jars, plates, etc. Exhibits this body of work one weekend at his house on Alice Street.

1967 *Shows for the first time with Wanda Hansen in San Francisco, with Stephen de Staebler and John Mason. Arneson makes his first bricks out of red terra-cotta imprinted with the name "Arneson." Summer: Shows for the first time at the San Francisco Museum of Modern Art in* Young California Artists. *David Gilhooly and Mel Ramos are included in this show, along with ten other artists. Receives appointment to the Institute of Creative Arts from the University of California. Spends the year in New York painting. Continues the Alice Street series and makes life-size paintings of the house. While teaching a summer course in Madison, Wisconsin, begins picture-frame series referencing popular historical styles in their decoration. Included in Peter Selz's show at U.C. Berkeley entitled* Funk.

1969 *Johnson Wax sponsors an exhibition entitled* Object U.S.A. *that includes several sculptures by Arneson. Johnson Wax buys a number of the works: a urinal, some of the Alice Street work, a sink, and Arneson's first self-portrait,* Self-Portrait of the Artist Losing His Marbles *from 1965. Included in* Human Concern, Personal Torment *at the Whitney Museum of American Art, New York. Begins making floor tiles for Alice Street home. The house catches fire (he used gasoline to remove mastic holding down the vinyl) and must be rebuilt. Collaborates with Roy de Forest on ceramic work, which they exhibit in Los Angeles at the Esther Robles Gallery in a show entitled* The Bob and Roy Show. *Participates in* Spirit of Comics *exhibition at the Institute of Contemporary Art at the University of Pennsylvania.*

1970 *Begins series of assembled cast-porcelain forms with printed letters based on the astrology chart machine at Grand Central Station. Exhibits at the Whitney Annual with five plates depicting a brick progressively sinking into a plate. This is the first year the Annual includes ceramicists. Takes a year off from teaching and moves temporarily to Benicia. Begins work based on the dinners he eats: the "Dirty Dish" series. Interest in illusion and foreshortening brings Arneson to construct a table using an advertisement from United Airlines which shows a chef standing over a long table of food. Includes a portrait of himself in chef's hat and titles the work* Smorgi-Bob, the Cook. *This begins Arneson's obsessive exploration of portraiture, both of himself and his friends.*

1971 *Arneson and Jeannette separate. Jeannette pursues graduate degree in art history. Arneson receives Artist's Fellowship from NEA. Arneson and Jeannette divorce; he has custody of the four boys.*

1972 *Exhibits at Hansen Fuller with eighteen self-portrait busts. Show sells out.*

1973 *Marries Sandra Shannonhouse, sculptor. Exhibits at the Cranbrook Academy of Art Gallery in Bloomfield Hills, Michigan, in a show entitled* Painting and Sculpture by Young American Artists. *Exhibits a urinal with female genitalia. Piece is installed in the basement of the museum behind a door. Appointed Professor at U. C. Davis.*

1974 *Museum of Contemporary Art in Chicago mounts a retrospective of Arneson's work curated by Stephen Prokopoff. Exhibition travels to the San Francisco Museum of Modern Art. Begins work on color lithography at Landfall Press in Chicago. This association will last for years; the first series of works is based on the "Dirty Dishes" sculpture series.*

1975 *First show at Allan Frumkin Gallery in New York. Receives excellent press but Arneson cannot attend: he has been diagnosed with cancer. Moves permanently to Benicia. He and Shannonhouse buy an old saloon and bordello and convert it into a home and studio. Begins working with "wet" glazes, making pools, water, and splashes.*

1977 *Frumkin exhibits busts of Arneson's friends: Roy de Forest, Allan Stone, David Gilhooly, Peter Voulkos.*

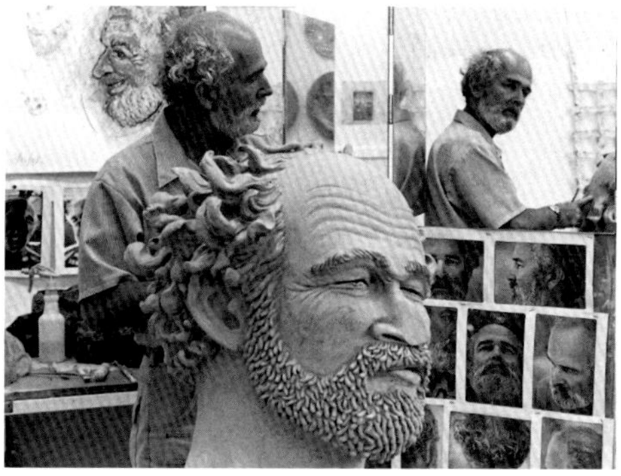

Robert Arneson in his studio with *Up Against It,* 1978

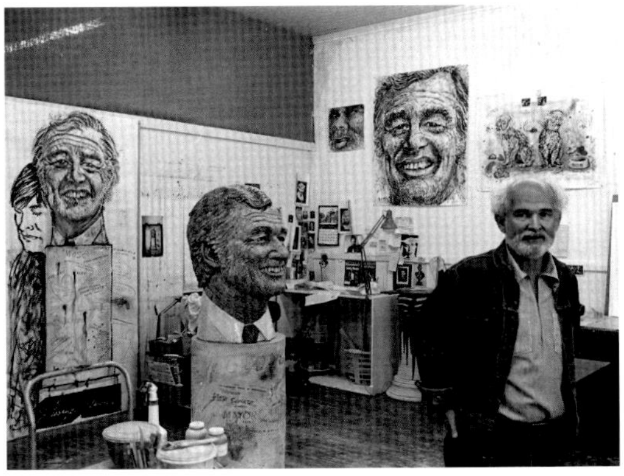

Robert Arneson in his studio with *Portrait of George* and related material, 1981

1978 *November 17: San Francisco Mayor George Moscone and Supervisor Harvey Milk are shot and killed by Supervisor Dan White. Six months later, White is found guilty of voluntary manslaughter rather than first degree murder. San Francisco erupts in violent protest. Arneson is awarded a National Endowment for the Arts grant.*

1978-81 *Arneson begins a series of works based on popular figures in modern art andpersonal heroes: Van Gogh, Picasso, Francis Bacon, Phillip Guston, and Marcel Duchamp. Revives a dormant genre of classical sculpture borrowed from ancient Rome by placing the busts on a pedestal, but demythifies the pedestal by including inscriptions and graffiti.*

1981 *Arneson submits proposal for bust of the late Mayor George Moscone, to be installed in the new Moscone Center in San Francisco. He is one of six artists chosen by the San Francisco Arts Commission to make work for the center. Included in exhibition* Ceramic Sculpture: Six Artists at the Whitney Museum. *Show travels to San Francisco Museum of Modern Art.*

1982 *November 29: Moscone bust* Portrait of George *installed at Moscone Center. December 2: Work is unveiled but pedestal remains draped at Mrs. Moscone's request; it contains controversial graffiti. Mayor Dianne Feinstein displays the pedestal for the press; great public outcry follows. December 6: The sculpture is removed from Moscone Center. Embittered by the events surrounding the Moscone bust, Arneson begins to address political and social issues in his art; starts a series of drawings on nuclear war images. The work initially focuses on victims of nuclear holocaust but moves on to include military machinery and leaders. Arneson undergoes an operation which seems to remove successfully the cancer he has been battling for over ten years.*

1983 *Arneson makes his first sculpture of Jackson Pollock while continuing the theme of nuclear war. Both subjects are to preoccupy him for years. Included in exhibition* Controversial Public Art *at the Milwaukee Art Museum, Wisconsin.*

1984 *Included in exhibition* The Shadow of the Bomb *at University Gallery, Amherst, Massachusetts, and Mt. Holyoke College Art Gallery.*

1985 *Awarded Honorary Doctor of Fine Arts, Rhode Island School of Design.*

1986 *Shannonhouse and Arneson's daughter, Tenaya, is born. The Des Moines Art Center mounts* Robert Arneson: A Retrospective, *curated by Neal Benezra, with major catalogue. Show travels to Hirshhorn Museum, Washington, D.C.; Portland Art Museum, Oregon; The Oakland Museum, California.*

1987 *Begins work on what he terms the "Myths of Western Man" series, as embodied by such public figures as Ronald Reagan and Jackson Pollock, and the process by which they are heroicized and sometimes victimized. Awarded Honorary Doctor of Fine Arts, San Francisco Art Institute.*

1989-90 *Series of sculptures, paintings, and drawings dealing with racism and class hatred, shown in* Robert Arneson: Black *at the Frumkin Gallery.*

1990 *In special tribute to Pollock, Arneson makes the huge sculpture* Guardians of the Secret II, *based on the painting* Guardians of the Secret *in the San Francisco Museum of Modern Art.*

1991 *In a group of wall reliefs comprised of multiple self-portraits, Arneson delves into challenging themes of disintegration of self, self-love, and self-hate. Series shown at Dorothy Goldeen Gallery, Los Angeles, and at Frumkin/Adams Gallery, New York, in 1992.*

1992 *Elected fellow, American Craft Council. Considerable body of work completed at Walla Walla Foundry in Washington, where Arneson had worked periodically for over ten years. A number of drawings and sculptures treat in harsh, graphic terms the effects of Arneson's chemotherapy treatments. Completes large outdoor bronze sculptures entitled* Egg Heads *commissioned for the campus of the University of California at Davis.*

November 2: Dies of cancer. The memorial service at Arneson's studio in Benicia draws many friends, colleagues, and admirers from around the country.

1993 *March. First posthumous show of Arneson's work at the John Berggruen Gallery in San Francisco. Includes bronzes and ceramic pieces based on themes from Brancusi and ancient architectural sculpture and the personal memorial,* Portrait at 62 Years.

Albright, Thomas. "In Memoriam, in Storage." *Art News* 81, no. 2 (February 1982): 13-14.

__________. *Art in the San Francisco Bay Area 1945-1980*. Berkeley and Los Angeles: University of California Press, 1985.

Adrian, Dennis. "Robert Arneson's Feats of Clay." *Art in America* 62, no. 5 (September-October 1974): 80-83.

Arneson, Robert. Interview by Mady Jones, August 1981. Archives of American Art, Smithsonian Institution.

__________. "Letters." *Artforum* 11, no. 4 (October 1963): 2.

Baker, Kenneth. "Arneson Takes on the Nuclear Threat." *San Francisco Chronicle* (9 November 1985): 36.

Ballatore, Sandy. "California Clay Rush." *Art in America* 64, no. 4 (July-August 1976): 84-88.

Benezra, Neal. *Robert Arneson: A Retrospective*. Exh. cat. Des Moines: Des Moines Art Center, 1986.

Berkson, Bill. "Robert Arneson: Fuller Goldeen Gallery." *Artforum* 24 (March 1986): 127.

Cameron, Dan. "Seven Types of Criticality." *Arts Magazine* 61, no. 9 (May 1987): 15-16.

Clark, Garth. *American Ceramics: 1876 to the Present*. Rev. ed. New York: Abbeville Press, 1987.

Clothier, Peter. "Robert Arneson: Goldeen." *Artnews* 87, no. 6 (Summer 1988): 201.

Coffelt, Beth. "Delta Bob and Captain Ace." *California Living. San Francisco Sunday Examiner and Chronicle* (8 April 1979): 40 47.

__________. "Arneson: Portrait/Self-Portraits," *Robert Arneson: Self-Portraits*. Exh. cat. Philadelphia: Moore College of Art, 1979.

Cummings, Paul. *Robert Arneson: Points of View*. Exh. cat. Pittsburgh: Pittsburgh Center for the Arts, 1986.

Doubet, Ward. "Robert Arneson: Portrait of the Artist as a Popular Iconoclast." *American Ceramics* 6, no. 1 (1987): 22-31.

Fineberg, Jonathan. *Robert Arneson: War Heads and Others*. Exh. cat. New York: Allan Frumkin Gallery, 1983.

__________. "Robert Arneson." *Robert Arneson: The Last Works*. Exh. cat. San Francisco: John Berggruen Gallery, 1993.

Frankenstein, Alfred. "Of Bricks, Pop Bottles, and a Better Mousetrap." *This World Magazine. San Francisco Sunday Examiner and Chronicle* (6 October 1974): 37-39.

__________. "The Ceramic Sculpture of Robert Arneson: Transforming Craft into Art." *Artnews* 75, no. 1 (January 1976): 48-50.

French, Christopher. "Raising the Stakes." *Artweek* 16, no. 38 (16 November 1985): 1.

Glueck, Grace. "A Partner to His Kiln." *New York Times* (15 May 1981): C21.

Hobbs, Robert, and Fredrick Woodard, eds. *Human Rights/Human Wrongs: Art and Social Change*. Iowa City: Museum of Art, University of Iowa, 1986.

__________. "Robert Arneson: Critic of Vanguard Extremism." *Arts Magazine* 62, no. 3 (November 1987): 88-93.

Hopkins, Henry, et al. *California Sculpture Show*. Exh. cat. Los Angeles: Fisher Gallery, University of Southern California, 1984.

Kelly, Ken. "Robert Arneson: The Interview." *San Francisco Focus* (October 1987): 42-58.

Kramer, Hilton. "Sculpture – From Boring to Brilliant," *New York Times* (15 May 1977): sec. 2, 27.

__________. "Ceramic Sculpture and the Taste of California," *New York Times* (20 December 1981): 31, 33.

Kuspit, Donald. "Arneson's Outrage." *Art in America* 73, no. 5 (May 1985): 134-139.

__________. *Robert Arneson*. Exh. cat. San Francisco: Fuller Goldeen Gallery, 1985.

__________. "Robert Arneson's Sense of Self: Squirming in Procrustean Place." *American Craft* 46, no. 5 (October-November 1986): 37-44, 64-68.

Marshall, Richard, and Suzanne Foley. *Ceramic Sculpture: Six Artists*. Exh. cat. New York: Whitney Museum of American Art, 1981.

McCann, Cecile. "About Arneson, Art and Ceramics." *Artweek* 5, no. 36 (26 October 1974): 1, 6-7.

McTwigan, Michael. *Robert Arneson: Heroes and Clowns*. Exh. cat. New York: Allan Frumkin Gallery, 1979.

__________. *Robert Arneson: New Ceramic Sculpture*. Exh. cat. New York: Allan Frumkin Gallery, 1981.

Miller-Keller, Andrea. *Robert Arneson / Matrix 110: From the Jackson Pollock Series*. Exh. brochure. Hartford: Wadsworth Atheneum, 1990.

Nixon, Bruce. *30 Years of TB-9: A Tribute to Robert Arneson*. Exh. cat. Davis, California: John Natsoulas Gallery, 1991.

Pohl, Frances. "Human Rights / Human Wrongs: Art and Social Change." Review. *Archives of American Art Journal* 28, no. 1 (1988): 26-30.

Prokopoff, Stephen, and Suzanne Foley. *Robert Arneson*. Exh. cat. Chicago: Museum of Contemporary Art, 1974.

Santiago, Chiori. "Robert Arneson: Oakland Museum." *Art News* 86, no. 5 (May 1987): 55-56.

Stich, Sidra. *Made in U.S.A.: An Americanization in Modern Art, The '50s & '60s*. Exh. cat. Berkeley: University Art Museum, University of California, 1987.

Summer, Robert. "Arneson's Bust." *Arts and Architecture* 1, no. 3 (August 1982): 14-16.

Thompson, Walter. "Robert Arneson at Frumkin." *Art in America* 76, no. 2 (February 1988): 149.

Yard, Sally. "The Shadow of the Bomb." *Arts Magazine* 58, no. 8 (April 1984): 73-82.

Yau, John. "Robert Arneson." *Artforum* 25, no. 3 (November 1986): 141-142.

Zack, David. "The Ceramics of Robert Arneson." *Craft Horizons* 30 (January-February 1970): 36ff.

Lenders to the Exhibition

Estate of the artist

Barbara and Gerson Bakar

John Berggruen Gallery

Patricia Bransten

Claire E. Flagg

Frumkin/Adams Gallery

Dorothy Goldeen Gallery

Foster Goldstrom

Brian Gross Fine Art, San Francisco

John Natsoulas Gallery

Rene di Rosa, Napa

The Runnymede Sculpture Farm,
founded by John and Dodie Rosekrans

San Francisco Museum of Modern Art

John and Earlene Taylor

Ross and Paula Turk

Riva Yares Gallery